The Smoky God
and other
Inner Earth
Mysteries

Edited by Timothy Green Beckley

Inner Light Publications

Composition and Layout:
Cross-Country Consultants
8858 E. Palm Ridge Drive
Scottsdale, AZ 85260

For foreign and reprint rights, contact:
Rights Department
Global Communications
Box 753
New Brunswick, NJ 08903

Introduction

by Timothy Green Beckley

Over the years, there has been a proven fascination with what may lay within the core of our own planet.

More than a hundred years ago, the famous science fiction writer Jules Verne wowed us with an eerie tale entitled *Journey to the Center of the Earth* (which was made into a Hollywood movie starring, of all people, Pat Boone). Though most of us would consider this work to be more of a novel than actual reality, the truth of the matter is–indeed–quite a bit more startling.

Around the same time that Verne's creation was originally printed, there was a strong belief among many that our planet was actually hollow and populated by a race of super beings. Many decades later, Hitler went afoul when he saw these entities as being part of an advanced "Arian Race" whom he hoped to communicate with.

Less known is a very rare manuscript that has been privately circulated for many years among metaphysical students, The Smoky God, which is presented as the true story of an individual who actually sailed into the Inner Earth and was befriended by giants the likes of whom have not walked on the outside of our planet since early Biblical times.

Now, Inner Light Publications is honored to present

not only this long scarce–and out of print–manuscript, but also, a totally new and valuable reference book that adds great light on what has often been presented as a very dark and "shadowy" subject.

Here–at last–is evidence that we do not have to look towards outer space for the origin of all UFOs, but that some "space ships" may be coming from a lot closer to home.

Read–Enjoy–Learn.

Tim Beckley
New Brunswick, NJ

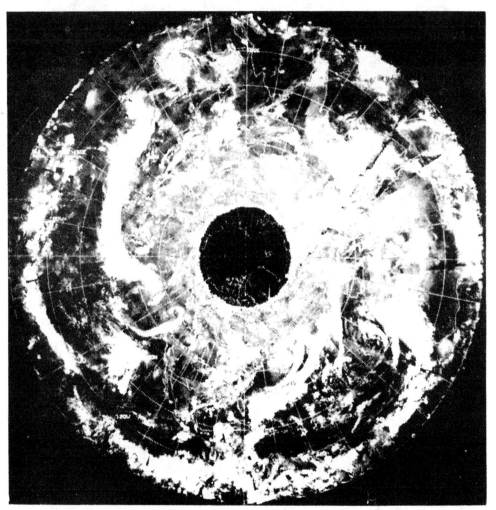

Taken from high above the Earth looking down, this rare photo released by NASA shows clearly the opening at the North Pole.

Contents

Artistic rendering of the "Holes at the Poles," along with the "central" sun at the core of the Inner Earth.

The Smoky God
Or
A Voyage to the Inner World

"He is the God who sits in the center, on the navel of the earth, and he is the interpreter of religion to all mankind."–PLATO

Part One
Author's Foreword

I FEAR the seemingly incredible story which I am about to relate will be regarded as the result of a distorted intellect superinduced, possibly, by the glamour of unveiling a marvelous mystery, rather than a truthful record of the unparalleled experiences related by one Olaf Jansen, whose eloquent madness so appealed to my imagination that all thought of an analytical criticism has been effectually dispelled.

Marco Polo will doubtless shift easily in his grave at the strange story I am called upon to chronicle; a story as strange as a Munchausen tale. It is also incongruous that I, a disbeliever, should be the one to edit the story of Olaf Jansen, whose name is now for the first time given to the world, yet who must hereafter rank as one of the notables of earth.

I freely confess his statements admit of no rational analysis, but have to do with the profound mystery concerning the frozen North that for centuries has claimed the attention of scientists and laymen alike.

However much they are at variance with the cosmographical manuscripts of the past, these plain statements may be relied upon as a record of the things Olaf Jansen claims to have seen with his own eyes.

A hundred times I have asked myself whether it is possible that the world's geography is incomplete, and that the startling narrative of Olaf Jansen is predicated upon demonstrable facts. The reader may be able to answer these queries to his own satisfaction, however far the chronicler of this narrative may be from having reached a conviction. Yet sometimes even I am at a loss to know whether I have been led away from an abstract truth by the *ignes fatui* of a clever superstition, or whether heretofore accepted facts are, after all, rounded upon falsity.

It may be that the true home of Apollo was not at Delphi, but in that older earth-center of which Plato speaks, where he says: "Apollo's real home is among the Hyperboreans, in a land of perpetual life, where mythology tells us two doves flying from the two opposite ends of the world met in this fair region, the home of Apollo. Indeed, according to Hecateeus, Leto, the mother of Apollo, was born on an island in the Arctic Ocean far beyond the North Wind."

It is not my intention to attempt a discussion of the theogony of the deities nor the cosmogony of the world. My simple duty is to enlighten the world concerning a heretofore unknown portion of the universe, as it was seen and described by the old Norseman, Olaf Jansen.

Interest in northern research is international. Eleven nations are engaged in, or have contributed to, the perilous work of trying to solve Earth's one remaining cosmological mystery.

There is a saying, ancient as the hills, that "truth is stranger than fiction," and in a most startling manner has this axiom been brought home to me within the last fortnight.

It was just two o'clock in the morning when I was aroused from a restful sleep by the vigorous ringing of my door-bell. The untimely disturber proved to be a messenger bearing a note, scrawled almost to the point of illegibility, from an old Norseman by the name of Olaf Jansen. After much deciphering, I made out the writing, which simply said: "Am ill unto death. Come." The call was imperative, and I lost no time in making ready to comply.

Perhaps I may as well explain here that Olaf Jansen, a man who quite recently celebrated his ninety-fifth birthday, has for the last half-dozen years been living alone in an unpretentious bungalow out Glendale way, a short distance from the business district of Los Angeles, California.

It was less than two years ago, while out walking one afternoon, that I was attracted by Olaf Jansen's house and its home-like surroundings, toward its owner and occupant, whom I afterward came to know as a believer in the ancient worship of Odin and Thor.

There was a gentleness in his face, and a kindly expression in the keenly alert gray eyes of this man who had lived more than four-score years and ten; and, withal, a sense of loneliness that appealed to my sympathy. Slightly stooped, and with his hands clasped behind him, he walked back and forth with slow and measured tread, that day when first we met. I can hardly say what particular motive impelled me to pause in my walk and engage him in conversation. He seemed pleased when I complimented him on the attractiveness of his bungalow, and on the well-tended vines and flowers clustering in profusion over its windows, roof and wide piazza.

I soon discovered that my new acquaintance was no ordinary person, but one profound and learned to a remarkable degree; a man who, in the later years of his long life, had dug deeply into books and become strong in the power of meditative silence.

I encouraged him to talk, and soon gathered that

he had resided only six or seven years in Southern California, but had passed the dozen years prior in one of the middle Eastern states. Before that he had been a fisherman off the coast of Norway, in the region of the Lofoden Islands, from whence he had made trips still farther north to Spitzbergen and even to Franz Josef Land.

When I started to take my leave, he seemed reluctant to have me go, and asked me to come again. Although at the time I thought nothing of it, I remember now that he made a peculiar remark as I extended my hand in leave-taking. "You will come again?" he asked. "Yes, you will come again some day. I am sure you will; and I shall show you my library and tell you many things of which you have never dreamed, things so wonderful that it may be you will not believe me."

I laughingly assured him that I would not only come again, but would be ready to believe whatever he might choose to tell me of his travels and adventures.

In the days that followed I became well acquainted with Olaf Jansen, and, little by little, he told me his story, so marvelous, that its very daring challenges reason and belief. The old Norseman always expressed himself with so much earnestness and sincerity that I became enthralled by his strange narrations.

Then came the messenger's call that night, and within the hour I was at Olaf Jansen's bungalow.

He was very impatient at the long wait, although after being summoned I had come immediately to his bedside.

"I must hasten," he exclaimed, while yet he held my hand in greeting. "I have much to tell you that you know not, and I will trust no one but you. I fully realize," he went on hurriedly, "that I shall not survive the night. The time has come to join my fathers in the great sleep."

12

I adjusted the pillows to make him more comfortable, and assured him I was glad to be able to serve him in any way possible, for I was beginning to realize the seriousness of his condition.

The lateness of the hour, the stillness of the surroundings, the uncanny feeling of being alone with the dying man, together with his weird story, all combined to make my heart beat fast and loud with a feeling for which I have no name. Indeed, there were many times that night by the old Norseman's couch, and there have been many times since, when a sensation rather than a conviction took possession of my very soul, and I seemed not only to believe in, but actually see, the strange lands, the strange people and the strange world of which he told, and to hear the mighty orchestral chorus of a thousand lusty voices.

For over two hours he seemed endowed with almost superhuman strength, talking rapidly, and to all appearances, rationally. Finally he gave into my hands certain data, drawings and crude maps. "These," said he in conclusion, "I leave in your hands. If I can have your promise to give them to the world, I shall die happy, because I desire that people may know the truth, for then all mystery concerning the frozen Northland will be explained. There is no chance of your suffering the fate I suffered. They will not put you in irons, nor confine you in a mad-house, because you are not telling your own story, but mine, and I, thanks to the gods, Odin and Thor, will be in my grave, and so beyond the reach of disbelievers who would persecute."

Without a thought of the far-reaching results the promise entailed, or foreseeing the many sleepless nights which the obligation has since brought me, I gave my hand and with it a pledge to discharge faithfully his dying wish.

13

As the sun rose over tile peaks of the San Jacinto, far to the eastward, the spirit of Olaf Jansen, the navigator, the explorer and worshiper of Odin and Thor, the man whose experiences and travels, as related, are without a parallel in all the world's history, passed away, and I was left alone with the dead.

And now, after having paid the last sad rites to this strange man from the Lofoden Islands, and the still farther "Northward Ho!", the courageous explorer of frozen regions, who in his declining years (after he had passed the four-score mark) had sought an asylum of restful peace in sunfavored California, I will undertake to make public his story.

But, first of all, let me indulge in one or two reflections:

Generation follows generation, and the traditions from the misty past are handed down from sire to son, but for some strange reason interest in the ice-locked unknown does not abate with the receding years, either in the minds of the ignorant or the tutored.

With each new generation a restless impulse stirs the hearts of men to capture the veiled citadel of the Arctic, the circle of silence, the land of glaciers, cold wastes of waters and winds that are strangely warm. Increasing interest is manifested in the mountainous icebergs, and marvelous speculations are indulged in concerning the earth's center of gravity, the cradle of the tides, where the whales have their nurseries, where the magnetic needle goes mad, where the Aurora Borealis illumines the night, and where brave and courageous spirits of every generation dare to venture and explore, defying the dangers of the "Farthest North."

One of the ablest works of recent years is *Paradise Found, or the Cradle of The Human Race at the North Pole,* by William F. Warren. In his carefully prepared volume, Mr. Warren almost stubbed his toe against the real truth, but missed it seemingly by only a hair's breadth, if the old Norseman's revelation be true.

Dr. Orville Livingston Leech, scientist, in a recent article, says:

"The possibilities of a land inside the earth were first brought to my attention when I picked up a geode on the shores of the Great Lakes. The geode is a spherical and apparently solid stone, but when broken is found to be hollow and coated with crystals. The earth is only a larger form of a geode, and the law that created the geode in its hollow form undoubtedly fashioned the earth in the same way."

In presenting the theme of this almost incredible story, as told by Olaf Jansen, and supplemented by manuscript, maps and crude drawings entrusted to me, a fitting introduction is found in the following quotation:

"In the beginning God created the heaven and the earth, and the earth was without form and void." And also, "God created man in his own image." Therefore, even in things material, man must be God-like, because he is created in the likeness of the Father.

A man builds a house for himself and family. The porches or verandas are all without, and are secondary. The building is really constructed for the conveniences within.

Olaf Jansen makes the startling announcement through me, an humble instrument, that in like manner, God created the earth for the "within"–that is to say, for its lands, seas, rivers, mountains, forests and valleys, and for its other internal conveniences, while the outside surface of the earth is merely the veranda, the porch, where things grow by comparison but sparsely, like the lichen on the mountain side, clinging determinedly for bare existence.

Take an egg-shell, and from each end break out a piece as large as the end of this pencil. Extract its contents, and then you will have a perfect representation of Olaf Jansen's earth. The distance from the inside surface to the outside surface, according to him, is about three hundred miles. The center of gravity is not in the center of the earth, but in the center of the shell or crust; therefore, if the thickness of the earth's crust or shell is three hundred miles, the center of gravity is one hundred and fifty miles below the surface.

In their log-books Arctic explorers tell us of the dipping of the needle as the vessel sails in regions of the farthest north known. In reality, they are at the curve; on the edge of the shell, where gravity is geometrically increased, and while the electric current seemingly dashes off into space toward the phantom idea of the North Pole, yet this same electric current drops again and continues its course southward along the inside surface of the earth's crust.

In the appendix to his work, Captain Sabine gives an account of experiments to determine the acceleration of the pendulum in different latitudes. This appears to have resulted from the joint labor of Peary and Sabine. He says: "The accidental discovery that a pendulum on being removed from Paris to the neighborhood of the equator increased its time of vibration, gave the first step to our present knowledge that the polar axis of the globe is less than the equatorial; that the force of gravity at the surface of the earth increases progressively from the equator toward the poles."

According to Olaf Jansen, in the beginning this old world of ours was created solely for the "within" world, where are located the four great rivers–the Euphrates, the Pison, the Gihon and the Hiddekel. These same names of rivers, when applied to streams on the "outside" surface of the earth are purely traditional from an antiquity beyond the memory of man.

On the top of a high mountain, near the fountainhead of these four rivers, Olaf Jansen, the Norseman, claims to have discovered the long-lost "Garden of Eden," the veritable navel of the earth, and to have spent over two years studying and reconnoitering in this marvelous "within" land, exuberant with stupendous plant life and abounding in giant animals; a land where the people live to be centuries old, after the order of Methuselah and other Biblical characters; a region where one-quarter of the "inner" surface is water and three-quarters land; where there are large oceans and many rivers and lakes; where the cities are superlative in construction and magnificence; where modes of transportation are as far in advance of ours as we with our boasted achievements are in advance of the inhabitants of "darkest Africa."

The distance directly across the space from inner surface to inner surface is about six hundred miles less than the recognized diameter of the earth. In the identical center of this vast vacuum is the seat of electricity–a mammoth ball of dull red fire–not startlingly brilliant, but surrounded by a white, mild, luminous cloud, giving out uniform warmth, and held in its place in the center of this internal space by the immutable law of gravitation. This electrical cloud is known to the people "within" as the abode of "The Smoky God." They believe it to be the throne of "The Most High."

Olaf Jansen reminded me of how, in the old college days, we were all familiar with the laboratory demonstrations of centrifugal motion, which clearly proved that, if the earth were a solid, the rapidity of its revolution upon its axis would tear it into a thousand fragments.

17

The old Norseman also maintained that from the farthest points of land on the islands of Spitzbergen and Franz Josef Land, flocks of geese may be seen annually flying still farther northward, just as the sailors and explorers record in their log-books. No scientist has yet been audacious enough to attempt to explain, even to his own satisfaction, toward what lands these winged fowls are guided by their subtle instinct. However, Olaf Jansen has given us a most reasonable explanation.

The presence of the open sea in the Northland is also explained. Olaf Jansen claims that the northern aperture, intake or hole, so to speak, is about fourteen hundred miles across. In connection with this, let us read what Explorer Nansen writes, on page 288 of his book: "I have never had such a splendid sail. On to the north, steadily north, with a good wind, as fast as steam and sail can take us, an open sea mile after mile, watch after watch, through these unknown regions, always clearer and clearer of ice, one might almost say: 'How long will it last?' The eye always turns to the northward as one paces the bridge. It is gazing into the future. But there is always the same dark sky ahead which means open sea." Again, the *Norwood Review* of England, in its issue of May 10, 1884, says: "We do not admit that there is ice up to the Pole once inside the great ice barrier, a new world breaks upon the explorer, the climate is mild like that of England, and, afterward, balmy as the Greek Isles."

Some of the rivers "within," Olaf Jansen claims, are larger than our Mississippi and Amazon rivers combined, in point of volume of water carried; indeed their greatness is occasioned by their width and depth rather than their length, and it is at the mouths of these mighty rivers, as they flow northward and southward

18

along the inside surface of the earth, that mammoth icebergs are found, some of them fifteen and twenty miles wide and from forty to one hundred miles in length.

Is it not strange that there has never been an iceberg encountered either in the Arctic or Antarctic Ocean that is not composed of fresh water ? Modern scientists claim that freezing eliminates the salt, but Olaf Jansen claims differently.

Ancient Hindoo, Japanese and Chinese writings, as well as the hieroglyphics of the extinct races of the North American continent, all speak of the custom of sun-worshiping, and it is possible, in the startling light of Olaf Jansen's revelations, that the people of the inner world, lured away by glimpses of the sun as it shone upon the inner surface of the earth, either from the northern or the southern opening, became dissatisfied with "The Smoky God," the great pillar or mother cloud of electricity, and, weary of their continuously mild and pleasant atmosphere, followed the brighter light, and were finally led beyond the ice belt and scattered over the "outer" surface of the earth, through Asia, Europe, North America and, later, Africa, Australia and South America.

The following quotation is significant; "It follows that man issuing from a mother-region still undetermined but which a number of considerations indicate to have been in the North, has radiated in several directions; that his migrations have been constantly from North to South."

(M. le Marquis G. de Saporta, in Popular Science Monthly, *October, 1883, page 753.)*

It is a notable fact that, as we approach the Equator, the stature of the human race grows less. But the Patagonians of South America are probably the only aborig-

19

ines from the center of the earth who came out through the aperture usually designated as the South Pole, and they are called the giant race.

Olaf Jansen avers that, in the beginning, the world was created by the Great Architect of the Universe, so that man might dwell upon its "inside" surface, which has ever since been the habitation of the "chosen." They who were driven out of the "Garden of Eden" brought their traditional history with them.

The history of the people living "within" contains a narrative suggesting the story of Noah and the ark with which we are familiar. He sailed away, as did Columbus, from a certain port, to a strange land he had heard of far to the northward, carrying with him all manner of beasts of the fields and fowls of the air, but was never heard of afterward.

On the northern boundaries of Alaska, and still more frequently on the Siberian coast, are found bone-yards containing tusks of ivory in quantities so great as to suggest the burying-places of antiquity. From Olaf Jansen's account, they have come from the great prolific animal life that abounds in the fields and forests and on the banks of numerous rivers of the Inner World. The materials were caught in the ocean currents, or were carried on ice-floes, and have accumulated like driftwood on the Siberian coast. This has been going on for ages, and hence these mysterious bone-yards.

On this subject William F. Warren, in his book already cited, pages 297 and 298, says: "The Arctic rocks tell of a lost Atlantis more wonderful than Plato's. The fossil ivory beds of Siberia excel everything of the kind in the world. From the days of Pliny, at least, they have constantly been undergoing exploitation, and still they are the chief headquarters of supply. The remains of mammoths are so abundant that, as Gratacap says, 'the northern islands of Siberia seem built up of crowded bones.' Another scientific writer, speaking of the islands of New Siberia, northward of the mouth of the River Lena, uses this language: 'Large quantities of ivory are dug out of the ground every year. Indeed, some of the islands are believed to be nothing but an accumulation of drift-timber and the bodies of mammoths and other antediluvian animals frozen together.' From this we may infer that, during the years that have elapsed since the Russian conquest of Siberia, useful tusks from more than twenty thousand mammoths have been collected."

But now for the story of Olaf Jansen. I give it in detail, as set down by himself in manuscript, and woven into the tale, just as he placed them, are certain quotations from recent works on Arctic exploration, showing how carefully the old Norseman compared with his own experiences those of other voyagers to the frozen North. Thus wrote the disciple of Odin and Thor.

"Twenty-eight years—long, tedious, frightful years of suffering.

Part Two
Olaf Jansen's Story

My name is Olaf Jansen. I am a Norwegian, although I was born in the little seafaring Russian town of Uleaborg, on the eastern coast of the Gulf of Bothnia, the northern arm of the Baltic Sea.

My parents were on a fishing cruise in the Gulf of Bothnia, and put into this Russian town of Uleaborg at the time of my birth, being the twenty-seventh day of October, 1811.

My father, Jens Jansen, was born at Rodwig on the Scandinavian coast, near the Lofoden Islands, but after marrying made his home at Stockholm, because my mother's people resided in that city. Then seven years old, I began going with my father on his fishing trips along the Scandinavian coast.

Early in life I displayed an aptitude for books, and at the age of nine years was placed in a private school in Stockholm, remaining there until I was fourteen. After this I made regular trips with my father on all his fishing voyages.

My father was a man fully six feet three in height, and weighed over fifteen stone, a typical Norseman of the most rugged sort, and capable of more endurance than any other man I have ever known. He possessed the gentleness of a woman in tender little ways, yet his

23

determination and will-power were beyond description. His will admitted of no defeat.

I was in my nineteenth year when we startled on what proved to be our last trip as fishermen, and which suited in the strange story that shall be given to the world,–but not until I have finished my earthly pilgrimage.

I dare not allow the facts as I know them to be published while I am living, for fear of further humiliation, confinement and suffering. First of all, I was put in irons by the captain of the whaling vessel that rescued me, for no other reason than that I told the truth about the marvelous discoveries made by my father and myself. But this was far from being the end of my tortures.

After four years and eight months' absence I reached Stockholm, only to find my mother had died the previous year, and the property left by my parents in the possession of my mother's people, but it was at once made over to me.

All might have been well, had I erased from my memory the story of our adventure and of my father's terrible death.

Finally, one day I told the story in detail to my uncle, Gustaf Osterlind, a man of considerable property, and urged him to fit out an expedition for me to make another voyage to the strange land.

At first I thought he favored my project. He seemed interested, and invited me to go before certain officials and explain to them, as I had to him, the story of our travels and discoveries. Imagine my disappointment and horror when, upon the conclusion of my narrative, certain papers were signed by my uncle, and, without warning, I found myself arrested and hurried away to dismal and fearful confinement in a madhouse, where

l remained for twenty-eight years–long, tedious, frightful years of suffering!

I never ceased to assert my sanity, and to protest
against the injustice of my confinement. Finally, on the
seventeenth of October, 1862, I was released. My uncle
was dead, and the friends of my youth were now
strangers. Indeed, a man over fifty years old, whose only
known record is that of a madman, has no friends.

I was at a loss to know what to do for a living, but
instinctively turned toward the harbor where fishing
boats in great numbers were anchored, and within a
week I had shipped with a fisherman by the name of
Yan Hansen, who was starting on a long fishing cruise
to the Lofoden Islands.

Here my earlier years of training proved of the very
greatest advantage, especially in enabling me to make
myself useful. This was but the beginning of other trips,
and by frugal economy I was, in a few years, able to
own a fishing-brig of my own.

For twenty-seven years thereafter I followed the sea
as a fisherman, five years working for others, and the
last twenty-two for myself.

During all these years I was a most diligent student
of books, as well as a hard worker at my business, but I
took greater care not to mention to anyone the story
concerning the discoveries made by my father and
myself. Even at this late day I would be fearful of having
any one see or know the things I am writing, and the
records and maps I have in my keeping. When my days
on earth are finished, I shall leave maps and records
that will enlighten and, I hope, benefit mankind.

The memory of my long confinement with mani-
acs, and all the horrible anguish and sufferings are too
vivid to warrant my taking further chances.

In 1889 I sold out my fishing boats, and found I had

accumulated a fortune quite sufficient to keep me the remainder of my life. I then came to America.

For a dozen years my home was in Illinois, near Batavia, where I gathered most of the books in my present library, though I brought many choice volumes from Stockholm. Later, I came to Los Angeles, arriving here March 4, 1901. The date I well remember, as it was President McKinley's second inauguration day. I bought this humble home and determined, here in the privacy of my own abode, sheltered by my own vine and fig-tree, and with my books about me, to make maps and drawings of the new lands we had discovered, and also to write the story in detail from the time my father and I left Stockholm until the tragic event that parted us in the Antarctic Ocean.

I well remember that we left Stockholm in our fishing-sloop on the third day of April, 1829, and sailed to the southward, leaving Gothland Island to the left and Oeland Island to the right. A few days later we succeeded in doubling Sandhommar Point, and made our way through the sound which separates Denmark from the Scandinavian coast. In due time we put in to the town of Christiansand, where we rested two days, and then started around the Scandinavian coast fo the westward, bound for the Lofoden Islands.

My father was in high spirit, because of the excellent and gratifying returns he had received from our last catch by marketing at Stockholm, instead of selling at one of the seafaring towns along the Scandinavian coast. He was especially pleased with the sale of some ivory tusks that he had found on the west coast of Franz Joseph Land during one of his northern cruises the previous year, and he expressed the hope that this time we might again be fortunate enough to load our little fishing-sloop with ivory, instead of cod, herring, mackerel

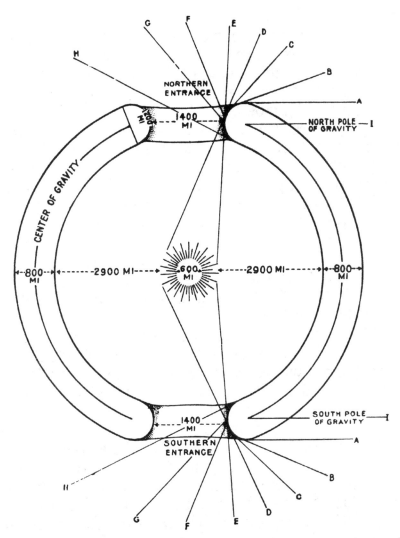

Diagram showing the earth as a hollow sphere with its polar openings and central sun. The letters at top and bottom of diagram indicate the various steps of an imaginary journey through the planet's interior. At the point marked "D," we catch our first glimpse of the corona of the central sun; at the point marked "E" we can see the central sun in its entirety.

27

and salmon.

We put in at Hammerfest, latitude seventy-one degrees and forty minutes, for a few days' rest. Here we remained one week, laying in an extra supply of provisions and several casks of drinking-water, and then sailed toward Spitzbergen.

For the first few days we had an open sea and a favoring wind, and then we encountered much ice and many icebergs. A vessel larger than our little fishing-sloop could not possibly have threaded its way among the labyrinth of icebergs or squeezed through the barely open channels. These monster bergs presented an endless succession of crystal palaces, of massive cathedrals and fantastic mountain ranges, grim and sentinellike, immovable as some towering cliff of solid rock, standing silent as a sphinx, resisting the restless waves of a fretful sea.

After many narrow escapes, we arrived at Spitzbergen on the 23rd of June, and anchored at Wijade Bay for a short time, where we were quite successful in our catches. We then lifted anchor and sailed through the Hinlopen Strait, and coasted along the North-East-Land.

A strong wind came up from the southwest, and my father said that we had better take advantage of it and try to reach Franz Josef Land, where, the year before he had, by accident, found the ivory tusks that had brought him such a good price at Stockholm.

It will be remembered that Andree started on his fatal balloon voyage from the northwest coast of Spitzbergen.

Never, before or since, have I seen so many sea-fowl; they were so numerous that they hid the rocks on the coast line and darkened the sky.

For several days we sailed along the rocky coast of Franz Josef Land. Finally, a favoring wind came up that enabled us to make the West Coast, and, after sailing twenty-four hours, we came to a beautiful inlet.

One could hardly believe it was the far Northland. The place was green with growing vegetation, and while the area did not comprise more than one or two acres, yet the air was warm and tranquil. It seemed to be at that point where the Gulf Stream's influence is most keenly felt.

On the east coast there were numerous icebergs, yet here we were in open water. Far to the west of us, however, were icepacks, and still farther to the westward the ice appeared like ranges of low hills. In front of us, and directly to the north, lay an open sea.

Sir John Barrow, Bart., F.R.S., in his work entitled "Voyages of Discovery and Research Within the Arctic Regions," says on page 57: "Mr. Beechey refers to what has frequently been found and noticed–the mildness of the temperature on the western coast of Spitzbergen, there being little or no sensation of cold, though the thermometer might be only a few degrees above the freezing-point. The brilliant and lively effect of a clear day, when the sun shines forth with a pure sky, whose azure hue is so intense as to find no parallel even in the boasted Italian sky."

My father was an ardent believer in Odin and Thor, and had frequently told me they were gods who came from far beyond the "North Wind." There was a tradition, my father explained, that still farther northward was a land more beautiful than any that mortal man had ever known, and that it was inhabited by the "Chosen."

Captain Kane, on page 299, quoting from Morton's Journal on Monday, the 26th of December, says: "As far as I could see, the open passages were fifteen miles or more wide, with sometimes mashed ice separating them. But it is all small ice, and I think it either drives out to the open space to the north or rots and sinks, as I could see none ahead to the north."

My youthful imagination was fired by the ardor, zeal and religious fervor of my good father, and I exclaimed: "Why not sail to this goodly land? The sky is fair, the wind favorable and the sea open."

We note the following in "Deutsche Mythologie," page 778, from the pen of Jakob Grimm; "There the sons of Bor built in the middle of the universe the city called Asgard, where dwell the gods and their kindred, and from that abode work out so many wondrous things both on the earth and in the heavens above it. There is in that city a place called Hlidskjalf, and when Odin is seated there upon his lofty throne he sees over the whole world and discerns all the actions of men."

Even now I can see the expression of pleasurable surprise on his countenance as he turned toward me and asked: "My son, are you willing to go with me and explore –to go far beyond where man has ever ventured?" I answered affirmatively. "Very well," he replied. "May the god Odin protect us!" and, quickly adjusting the sails, he glanced at our compass, turned the prow in due northerly direction through an open channel, and our voyage had begun.

Hall writes, on page 288: "On the 23rd of January, the two Esquimaux, accompanied by two of the seamen, went to Cape Lupton. They reported a sea of open water extending as far as the eye could reach."

The sun was low in the horizon, as it was still the early summer. Indeed, we had almost four months of day ahead of us before the frozen night could come on again.

Our little fishing-sloop sprang forward as if eager as ourselves for adventure. Within thirty-six hours we were out of sight of the highest point on the coast line of Franz Josef Land. We seemed to be in a strong current running north by northeast. Far to the right and to the left of us were icebergs, but our little sloop bore down on the narrows and passed through channels and out into open seas –channels so narrow in places that, had our craft been other than small, we never could have gotten through.

On the third day we came to an island. Its shores were washed by an open sea. My father determined to land and explore for a day. This new land was destitute of timber, but we found a large accumulation of drift-wood on the northern shore. Some of the trunks of the trees were forty feet long and two feet in diameter.

Greely tells us in vol. 1, page 100, that: "Privates Connell and Frederick found a large coniferous tree on the beach, just above the extreme high-water mark. It was nearly thirty inches in circumference, some thirty feet long, and had apparently been carried to that point by a current within a couple of years. A portion of it was cut up for fire-wood, and for the first time in that valley, a bright, cheery campfire gave comfort to man."

After one day's exploration of the coast line of this island, we lifted anchor and turned our prow to the north in an open sea.

I remember that neither my father nor myself had tasted food for almost thirty hours. Perhaps this was because of the tension of excitement about our strange voyage in waters farther north, my father said, than anyone had ever before been. Active mentality had dulled the demands of the physical needs.

Dr. Kane says, on page 379 of his works: "I cannot imagine what becomes of the ice. A strong current sets in constantly to the north; but, from altitudes of more than five hundred feet, I saw only narrow strips of ice, with great spaces of open water, from ten to fifteen miles in breadth, between them. It must, therefore, either go to an open space in the north, or dissolve."

Instead of the cold being intense as we had anticipated, it was really warmer and more pleasant than it had been while in Hammerfest on the north coast of Norway, some six weeks before.

Captain Peary's second voyage relates another circumstance which may serve to confirm a conjecture which has long been maintained by some, that an open sea, free of ice, exists at or near the Pole. "On the second of November," says Peary, "the wind freshened up to a gale from north by west, lowered the thermometer before midnight to 5 degrees, whereas, a rise of wind at Melville Island was generally accompanied by a simultaneous rise in the thermometer at low temperatures. May not this," he asks, "be occasioned by the wind blowing over an open sea in the quarter from which the wind blows? And tend to confirm the opinion that at or near the Pole an open sea exists?"

We both frankly admitted that we were very hungry, and forthwith I prepared a substantial meal from our well-stored larder. When we had partaken heartily of the repast, I told my father I believed I would sleep, as I was beginning to feel quite drowsy. "Very well," he replied, "I will keep the watch."

I have no way to determine how long I slept; I only know that I was rudely awakened by a terrible commotion in the sloop. To my surprise, I found my father sleeping soundly. I cried out lustily to him, and starting up, he sprang quickly to his feet. Indeed, had he not instantly clutched the rail, he would certainly have been thrown into the seething waves.

A fierce snow-storm was raging. The wind was directly astern, driving our sloop at terrific speed, and was threatening every moment to capsize us. There was no time to lose, the sails had to be lowered immediately. Our boat was writhing in convulsions. A few icebergs we knew were on either side of us, but fortunately the channel was open directly to the north. But would it remain so? In front of us, girding the horizon from left to right, was a vaporish fog or mist, black as Egyptian night at the water's edge, and white like a steam-cloud toward the top, which was finally lost to view as it blended with the great white flakes of falling snow. Whether it covered a treacherous iceberg, or some other hidden obstacle against which our little sloop would dash and send us to a watery grave, or was merely the phenomenon of an Arctic fog, there was no way to determine.

On page 284 of his works, Hall writes: "From the top of Providence Berg, a dark fog was seen to the north, indicating water. At 10 a.m. three of the men (Kruger, Nindemann and Hobby) went to Cape Lupron to ascertain if possible the extent of the open water. On their return they reported several open spaces and much young ice–not more than a day old, so thin that it was easily broken by throwing pieces of ice upon it."

By what miracle we escaped being dashed to utter destruction, I do not know. I remember our little craft creaked and groaned, as if its joints were breaking. It rocked and staggered to and fro as if clutched by some fierce undertow of whirlpool or maelstrom.

Fortunately our compass had been fastened with long screws to a crossbeam. Most of our provisions, however, were tumbled out and swept away from the deck of the cuddy, and had we not taken the precaution at the very beginning to tie ourselves firmly to the masts of the sloop, we should have been swept into the lashing sea.

Above the deafening tumult of the raging waves, I

33

It was not uncommon for sailors at sea to report a mysterious aerial glow near the entranceways at the North and South Poles.

heard my father's voice. "Be courageous, my son," he shouted, "Odin is the god of the waters, the companion of the brave, and he is with us. Fear not."

To me it seemed there was no possibility of our escaping a horrible death. The little sloop was shipping water, the snow was falling so fast as to be blinding, and the waves were tumbling over our counters in reckless white-sprayed fury. There was no telling what instant we should be dashed against some drifting ice-pack. The tremendous swells would heave us up to the very peaks of mountainous waves, then plunge us down into the depths of the sea's trough as if our fishing-sloop were a fragile shell. Gigantic white-capped waves, like veritable walls, fenced us in, fore and aft.

This terrible nerve-racking ordeal, with its nameless horrors of suspense and agony of fear indescribable, continued for more than three hours, and all the time we were being driven forward at fierce speed. Then suddenly, as if growing weary of its frantic exertions, the wind began to lessen its fury and by degrees to die down.

At last we were in a perfect calm. The fog mist had also disappeared, and before us lay an iceless channel perhaps ten or fifteen miles wide, with a few icebergs far away to our right, and an intermittent archipelago of smaller ones to the left.

I watched my father closely, determined to remain silent until he spoke. Presently he untied the rope from his waist and, without saying a word, began working the pumps, which fortunately were not damaged, relieving the sloop of the water it had shipped in the madness of the storm.

He put up the sloop's sails as calmly as if casting a fishing-net, and then remarked that we were ready for a favoring wind when it came. His courage and persistence were truly remarkable.

On investigation we found less than one-third of our provisions remaining, while to our utter dismay, we discovered that our water-casks had been swept overboard during the violent plungings of our boat.

Two of our water-casks were in the main hold, but both were empty. We had a fair supply of food, but no fresh water. I realized at once the awfulness of our position. Presently I was seized with a consuming thirst.' "It is indeed bad," remarked my father. "However, let us dry our bedraggled clothing, for we are soaked to the skin. Trust to the god Odin, my son. Do not give up hope."

The sun was beating down slantingly, as if we were in a southern latitude, instead of in the far Northland. It was swinging around, its orbit ever visible and rising higher and higher each day, frequently mist-covered, yet always peering through the lacework of clouds like some fretful eye of fate, guarding the mysterious Northland and jealously watching the pranks of man. Far to our right the rays decking the prisms of icebergs were gorgeous. Their reflections emitted flashes of garnet, of diamond, of sapphire. A pyrotechnic panorama of countless colors and shapes, while below could be seen the green-tinted sea, and above, the purple sky.

"It could hardly be said to resemble the sun except in its circular shape."

Part Three
Beyond the North Wind

I TRIED to forget my thirst by busying myself with bringing up some food and an empty vessel from the hold. Reaching over the siderail, I filled the vessel with water for the purpose of laving my hands and face. To my astonishment, when the water came in contact with my lips, I could taste no salt. I was startled by the discovery. "Father !" I fairly gasped, "the water, the water; it is fresh!" "What, Olaf!" exclaimed my father glancing hastily around. "Surely you are mistaken. There is no land. You are going mad." "But taste it!" I cried.

And thus we made the discovery that the water was indeed fresh, absolutely so, without the least briny taste or even the suspicion of a salty flavor.

We forthwith filled our two remaining water-casks, and my father declared it was a heavenly dispensation of mercy from the gods Odin and Thor.

We were almost beside ourselves with joy, but hunger bade us end enforced fast. Now that we had found fresh water in the open sea, what might we not expect in this strange latitude where ship had never before sailed and the splash of an oar had never been heard?

We had scarcely appeased our hunger when a breeze began filling the idle sails, and, glancing at the compass, we found the northern point pressing hard against the glass.

In vol. I, page 196, Nansen writes: "It is a peculiar phenomenon–this dead water. We had at present a better opportunity of studying it than we desired. It occurs where a surface layer of fresh water rests upon the salt water of the sea, and this fresh water is carried along with the ship gliding on the heavier sea beneath it as if on a fixed foundation. The difference between the two strata was in this case so great that, while we had drinking water on the surface, the water we got from the bottom cock of the engine-room was far too salty to be used for the boiler."

In response to my surprise, my father said, "I have heard of this before; it is what they call the dipping of the needle."

We loosened the compass and turned it at right angles with the surface of the sea before its point would free itself from the glass and point according to unmolested attraction. It shifted uneasily, and seemed as unsteady. as a drunken man, but finally pointed a course.

Before this we thought the wind was carrying us north by northwest, but, with the needle free, we discovered, if it could be relied upon, that we were sailing slightly north by northeast. Our course, however, was ever tending northward.

In volume 11, pages 18 and 19, Nansen writes about the inclination of the needle. Speaking of Johnson, his aide: "One day–it was November 24th–he came in to supper a little after six o'clock, quite alarmed, and said: 'There has just been a singular inclination of the needle in twenty-four degrees. And remarkably enough, its northern extremity pointed to the east.'"

We again find in Peary's first voyage–page 67,–the

following: "*It had been observed that from the moment they had entered Lancaster Sound, the motion of the compass needle was very sluggish, and both this and its deviation increased as they progressed to the westward, and continued to do so in descending this inlet. Having reached latitude 73 degrees, they witnessed for the first time the curious phenomenon of the directive power of the needle becoming so weak as to be completely overcome by the attraction of the ship, so that the needle might now be said to point to the north pole of the ship.*"

The sea was serenely smooth, with hardly a choppy wave, and the wind brisk and exhilarating. The sun's rays, while striking us aslant, furnished tranquil warmth. And thus time wore on day after day, and we found from the record in our logbook, we had been sailing eleven days since the storm in the open sea.

By strictest economy, our food was holding out fairly well, but beginning to run low. In the meantime, one of our casks of water had been exhausted, and my father said: "We will fill it again." But, to our dismay, we found the water was now as salty as in the region of the Lofoden Islands off the coast of Norway. This necessitated our being extremely careful of the remaining cask.

I found myself wanting to sleep much of the time; whether it was the effect of the exciting experience of sailing in unknown waters, or the relaxation from the awful excitement incident to our adventure in a storm at sea, or due to want of food, I could not say.

I frequently lay down on the bunker of our little sloop, and looked far up into the blue dome of the sky; and, notwithstanding the sun was shining far away in the east, I always saw a single star overhead. For several days, when I looked for this star, it was always there directly above us.

It was now, according to our reckoning, about the first of August. The sun was high in the heavens, and was so bright that I could no longer see the one lone star that attracted my attention a few days earlier.

One day about this time, my father startled me by calling my attention to a novel sight far in front of us, almost at the horizon. "It is a mock sun," exclaimed my father. "I have read of them; it is called a reflection or mirage. It will soon pass away."

But this dull-red, false sun, as we supposed it to be, did not pass away for several hours; and while we were unconscious of its emitting any rays of light, still there was no time thereafter when we could not sweep the horizon in front and locate the illumination of the so-called false sun, during a period of at least twelve hours out of every twenty-four.

Clouds and mists would at times almost, but never entirely, hide its location. Gradually it seemed to climb higher in the horizon of the uncertain purply sky as we advanced.

It could hardly be said to resemble the sun, except in its circular shape, and when not obscured by clouds or the ocean mists, it had a hazy-red, bronzed appearance, which would change to a white light like a luminous cloud, as if reflecting some greater light beyond.

We finally agreed in our discussion of this smoky furnace-colored sun, that, whatever the cause of the phenomenon, it was not a reflection of our sun, but a planet of some sort–a reality.

Nansen, on page 394, says: "Today another noteworthy thing happened, which was that about midday we saw the sun, or to be more correct, an image of the sun, for it was only a mirage. A peculiar impression was produced by the sight of that glowing fire lit just

41

above the outermost edge of the ice. According to the enthusiastic descriptions given by many Arctic travelers of the first appearance of this god of life after the long winter night, the impression ought to be one of jubilant excitement; but it was not so in my case. We had not expected to see it for some days yet, so that my feeling was rather one of pain, of disappointment, that we must have drifted farther south than we thought. So it was with pleasure that I soon discovered that it could not be the sun itself. The mirage was at first a flattened-out, glowing red streak of fire on the horizon; later there were two streaks, the one above the other, with a dark space between; and from the maintop I could see four, or even five, such horizontal lines directly over one another, all of equal length, as if one could only imagine a square, dull-red sun, with horizontal dark streaks across it."

One day soon after this, I felt exceedingly drowsy, and fell into a sound sleep. But it seemed that I was almost immediately aroused by my father's vigorous shaking of me by the shoulder and saying: "Olaf, awaken; there is land in sight!"

I sprang to my feet, and oh! joy unspeakable! There, far in the distance, yet directly in our path, were lands jutting boldly into the sea. The shore-line stretched far away to the right of us, as far as the eye could see, and all along the sandy beach were waves breaking into choppy foam, receding, then going forward again, ever chanting in monotonous thunder tones the song of the deep. The banks were covered with trees and vegetation.

I cannot express my feeling of exultation at this discovery. My father stood motionless, with his hand on the tiller, looking straight ahead, pouring out his heart in thankful prayer and thanksgiving to the gods Odin and Thor.

In the meantime, a net which we found in the stowage had been cast, and we caught a few fish that materially added to our dwindling stock of provisions.

The compass, which we had fastened back in its place, in fear of other storm, was still pointing due north, and moving on its pivot, just as it had at Stockholm. The dipping of the needle had ceased. What could this mean? Then, too, our many days of sailing had certainly carried us far past the North Pole. And yet the needle continued to point north. We were sorely perplexed, for surely our direction was now south.

We sailed for three days along the shoreline, then came to the mouth of a fjord or river of immense size. It seemed more like a great bay, and into this we turned our fishing-craft, the direction being slightly northeast of south. By the assistance of a fretful wind that came to our aid about twelve hours out of every twenty four, we continued to make our way inland, into what afterward proved to be a mighty river, and which we learned was called by the inhabitants Hiddekel.

Peary's first voyage, pages 69 and 70, says: "On reaching Sir Byam Martin's Island, the nearest to Melville Island, the latitude of the place of observation was 75 degrees–09'–23", and the longitude 103 degrees-44'-37"; the dip of the magnetic needle 88 degrees-25'-58" west in the longitude of 91 degrees-48', where the last observations on the shore had been made, to 165 degrees-50'-09", east, at their present station, so that we had," says Peary, "in sailing over the space included between these two meridians, crossed immediately northward of the magnetic pole, and had undoubtedly passed over one of those spots upon the globe where the needle would have been found to vary 180 degrees, or in other words, where the North Pole would have pointed to the south."

We continued our journey for ten days thereafter, and found we had fortunately attained a distance inland where ocean tides no longer affected the water, which had become fresh.

The discovery came none to soon, for our remaining cask of water was well-nigh exhausted. We lost no time in replenishing our casks, and continued to sail farther up the river when the wind was favorable.

Along the banks great forests miles in extent could be seen stretching away on the shore-line. The trees were of enormous size. We landed after anchoring, near a sandy beach, and waded ashore, and were rewarded by finding a quantity of nuts that were very palatable and satisfying to hunger, and a welcome change from the monotony of our stock of provisions.

It was about the first of September, over five months, we calculated, since our leave-taking from Stockholm. Suddenly we were frightened almost out of our wits by hearing in the far distance the singing of people. Very soon thereafter we discovered a huge ship gliding down the river directly toward us. Those aboard were singing in one mighty chorus that, echoing from bank to bank, sounded like a thousand voices, filling the whole universe with quivering melody. The accompaniment was played on stringed instruments not unlike our harps.

It was a larger .ship than any we had ever seen, and was differently constructed.

Asiatic Mythology,–page 240, "Paradise Found"– from translation by Sayce, in a book called "Records of the Past," we were told of a "dwelling" which "the gods created for" the first human beings,–a dwelling in which they "became great" and "increased in numbers," and the location of which is described in words exactly corresponding to those of Iranian, Indian, Chi-

nese, Eddaic and Aztecan literature; namely, "in the center of the earth."—Warren

At this particular time our sloop was becalmed, and not far from the shore. The bank of the river, covered with mammoth trees, rose up several hundred feet in beautiful fashion. We seemed to be on the edge of some primeval forest that doubtless stretched far inland.

The immense craft paused, and almost immediately a boat was lowered and six men of gigantic stature rowed to our little fishing-sloop. They spoke to us in a strange language. We knew from their manner, however, that they were not unfriendly. They talked a great deal among themselves, and one of them laughed immoderately, as though in finding us a queer discovery had been made. One of them spied our compass, and it seemed to interest them more than any other part of our sloop.

Finally, the leader motioned as if to ask whether we were willing to leave our craft to go on board their ship. "What say you, my son?" asked my father. "They cannot do any more than kill us."

"They seem to be kindly disposed," I replied, "although what terrible giants! They must be the select six of the kingdom's crack regiment. Just look at their great size."

"We may as well go willingly as be taken by force," said my father, smiling, "for they are certainly able to capture us." Thereupon he made known, by signs, that we were ready to accompany them.

Within a few minutes we were on board the ship, and half an hour later our little fishing-craft had been lifted bodily out of the water by a strange sort of hook and tackle, and set on board as a curiosity.

There were several hundred people on board this,

"They spoke to us in a strange language."

to us, mammoth ship, which we discovered was called "The Naz," meaning, as we afterward learned, "Pleasure," or to give a more proper interpretation, "Pleasure Excursion" ship.

If my father and I were curiously observed by the ship's occupants, this strange race of giants offered us an equal amount of wonderment.

There was not a single man aboard who would not have measured fully twelve feet in height. They all wore full beards, not particularly long, but seemingly short-cropped. They had mild and beautiful faces, exceedingly fair, with ruddy complexions. The hair and beard of some were black, others sandy, and still others yellow. The captain, as we designated the dignitary in command of the great vessel, was fully a head taller than any of his companions. The women averaged from ten to eleven feet in height. Their features were especially regular and refined, while their complexion was of a most delicate tint heightened by a healthful glow.

Both men and women seemed to possess that particular ease of manner which we deem a sign of good breeding, and, notwithstanding their huge statures, there was nothing about them suggesting awkwardness. As I was a lad in only my nineteenth year, I was doubtless looked upon as a true Tom Thumb. My father's six feet three did not lift the top of his head above the waist line of these people.

According to all procurable data, that spot at the era of male's appearance upon the stage was in the now lost 'Miocene continent,' which then surrounded the Arctic Pole. That in that true, original Eden some of the early generations of men attained to a stature and longevity unequaled in any countries known to post-diluviarn history is by no means scientifically incredible."–Wm. F. Warrens, "Paradise Found," p. 284.

Each one seemed to vie with the others in extending courtesies and showing kindness to us, but all laughed heartily, I remember, when they had to improvise chairs for my father and myself to sit at table. They were richly attired in a costume peculiar to themselves, and very attractive. The men were clothed in handsomely embroidered tunics of silk and satin and belted at the waist. They wore knee-breeches and stockings of a fine texture, while their feet were encased in sandals adorned with gold buckles. We early discovered that gold was one of the most common metals known, and that it was used extensively in decoration.

Strange as it may seem, neither my father nor myself felt the least bit of solicitude for our safety. "We have come into our own," my father said to me. "This is the fulfillment of the tradition told me by my father and my father's father, and still back for many generations of our race. This is, assuredly, the land beyond the North Wind."

We seemed to make such an impression on the party that we were given specially into the charge of one of the men, Jules Galdea, and his wife, for the purpose of being educated in their language; and we, on our part, were just as eager to learn as they were to instruct.

At the captain's command, the vessel was swung cleverly about, and began retracing its course up the river. The machinery, while noiseless, was very powerful.

The banks and trees on either side seemed to rush by. The ship's speed, at times, surpassed that of any railroad train on which I have ever ridden, even here in America. It was wonderful.

In the meantime we had lost sight of the sun's rays, but we found a radiance "within" emanating from the dull-red sun which had already attracted our attention, now giving out a white light seemingly from a cloud-bank far away in front of us. It dispensed a greater light, I should say, than two full moons on the clearest night.

In twelve hours this cloud of whiteness would pass out of sight as if eclipsed, and the twelve hours following corresponded with our night. We early learned that these strange people were worshipers of this great cloud of night. It was "The Smoky God" of the "Inner World."

The ship was equipped with a mode of illumination which I now presume was electricity, but neither my father nor myself were sufficiently skilled in mechanics to understand whence came the power to operate the ship, or to maintain the soft beautiful lights that answered the same purpose of our present methods of lighting the streets of our cities, our houses and places of business.

It must be remembered, the time of which we write was the autumn of 1829, and we of the "outside" surface of the earth knew nothing then, so to speak, of electricity.

The electrically surcharged condition of the air was a constant vitalizer. I never felt better in my life than during the two years my father and I sojourned on the inside of the earth.

To resume my narrative of events: The ship on which we were sailing came to a stop two days after we had been taken on board. My father said as nearly as he could judge, we were directly under Stockholm or London.

The city we had reached was called "Jehu," signifying a seaport town. The houses were large and beautifully constructed, and quite uniform in appearance, yet without sameness. The principal occupation of the people appeared to be agriculture; the hillsides were

49

covered with vineyards, while the valleys were devoted to the growing of grain.

I never saw such a display of gold. It was everywhere. The door-casings were inlaid and the tables were veneered with sheetings of gold. Domes of the public buildings were of gold. It was used most generously in the finishings of the great temples of music.

Vegetation grew in lavish exuberance, and fruit of all kinds possessed the most delicate flavor. Clusters of grapes four and five feet in length, each grape as large as an orange, and apples larger than a man's head typified the wonderful growth of all things on the 'inside" of the earth.

The great redwood trees of California would be considered mere underbrush compared with the giant forest trees extending for miles and miles in all directions. In many directions along the foothills of the mountains vast herds of cattle were seen during the last day of our travel on the river.

We heard much of a city called "Eden," but were kept at "Jehu" for an entire year. By the end of that time we had learned to speak fairly well the language of this strange race of people. Our instructors, Jules Galdea and his wife, exhibited a patience that was truly commendable.

One day an envoy from the Ruler at "Eden" came to see us, and for two whole days my father and myself were put through a series of surprising questions. They wished to know from whence we came, what sort of people dwelt "without," what God we worshiped, our religious beliefs, the mode of living in our strange land, and a thousand other things.

The compass which we had brought with us attracted especial attention. My father and I commented between ourselves on the fact that the compass still pointed north, although we now knew that we had sailed over the curve or edge of the earth's aperture, and were far along southward on the "inside" surface of the earth's crust, which, according to my father's estimate and my own, is about three hundred miles in thickness from the "inside" to the "outside" surface. Relatively speaking, it is no thicker than an egg-shell, so that there is almost as much surface on the "inside" as on the "outside" of the earth.

The great luminous cloud or ball of dull-red fire-fiery-red in the mornings and evenings, and during the day giving off a beautiful white light, "The Smoky God," –is seemingly suspended in the center of the great vacuum "within" the earth, and held to its place by the immutable law of gravitation, or a repellent atmospheric force, as the case may be. I refer to the known power that draws or repels with equal force in all directions.

The base of this electrical cloud or central luminary, the seat of the gods, is dark and non-transparent, save for innumerable small openings, seemingly in the bottom of the great support or altar of the Deity, upon which "The Smoky God" rests; and, the lights shining through these many openings twinkle at night in all their splendor, and seem to be stars, as natural as the stars we saw shining when in our home at Stockholm, excepting that they appear larger. "The Smoky God," therefore, with each daily revolution of the earth, appears to come up in the east and go down in the west, the same as does our sun on the external surface. In reality, the people "within" believe that "The Smoky God" is the throne of their Jehovah, and is stationary. The effect of night and day is, therefore, produced by the earth's daily rotation.

I have since discovered that the language of the people of the Inner World is much like the Sanskrit.

After we had given an account of ourselves to the emissaries from the central seat of government of the inner continent, and my father had, in his crude way, drawn maps, at their request, of the "outside" surface of the earth, showing the divisions of land and water, and giving the name of each of the continents, large islands and the oceans, we were taken overland to the city of "Eden," in a conveyance different from anything we have in Europe or America. This vehicle was doubtless some electrical contrivance. It was noiseless, and ran on a single iron rail in perfect balance. The trip was made at a very high rate of speed. We were carried up hills and down dales, across valleys and again along the sides of steep mountains, without any apparent attempt having been made to level the earth as we do for railroad tracks. The car seats were huge yet comfortable affairs, and very high above the floor of the car. On the top of each car were high geared fly wheels lying on their sides, which were so automatically adjusted that, as the speed of the car increased, the high speed of these fly wheels geometrically increased. Jules Galdea explained to us that these revolving fan-like wheels on top of the cars destroyed atmospheric pressure, or what is generally understood by the term gravitation, and with this force thus destroyed or rendered nugatory the car is as safe from falling to one side or the other from the single rail track as if it were in a vacuum; the fly wheels in their rapid revolutions destroying effectually the so-called power of gravitation, or the force of atmospheric pressure or whatever potent influence it may be that causes all unsupported things to fall downward to the earth's surface or to the nearest point of resistance.

The surprise of my father and myself was indescribable when, amid the regal magnificence of a spacious hall, we were finally brought before the Great

High Priest, ruler over all the land. He was richly robed, and much taller than those about him, and could not have been less than fourteen or fifteen feet in height. The immense room in which we were received seemed finished in solid slabs of gold thickly studded with jewels of amazing brilliancy.

The city of "Eden" is located in what seems to be a beautiful valley, yet, in fact, it is on the loftiest mountain plateau of the Inner Continent, several thousand feet higher than any portion of the surrounding country. It is the most beautiful place I have ever beheld in all my travels. In this elevated garden all manner of fruits, vines, shrubs, trees, and flowers grow in riotous profusion.

In this garden four rivers have their source in a mighty artesian fountain. They divide and flow in four directions. This place is called by the inhabitants the "navel of the earth," or the beginning, "the cradle of the human race." The names of the rivers are the Euphrates, the Pison, the Gihon, and the Hiddekel.

"And the Lord God planted a garden, and out of the ground made the Lord God to grow every tree that is pleasant to the sight and good for food."–The Book of Genesis.

The unexpected awaited us in this palace of beauty, in the finding of our little fishing-craft. It had been brought before the High Priest in perfect shape, just as it had been taken from the waters that day when it was loaded on board the ship by the people who discovered us on the river more than a year before.

We were given an audience of over two hours with this great dignitary, who seemed kindly disposed and considerate. He showed himself eagerly interested, asking us numerous questions, and invariably regarding things about which his emissaries had failed to inquire.

At the conclusion of the interview he inquired our

"We were brought before the Great High Priest."

pleasure, asking us whether we wished to remain in his country or if we preferred to return to the "outer" world, providing it were possible to make a successful return trip, across the frozen belt barriers that encircle both the northern and southern openings of the earth.

My father replied: "It would please me and my son to visit your country and see your people, your colleges and palaces of music and art, your great fields, your wonderful forests of timber; and after we have had this pleasurable privilege, we should like to try to return to our home on the 'outside' surface of the earth. This son is my only child, and my good wife will be weary awaiting our return."

"I fear you can never return," replied the Chief High Priest, "because the way is a most hazardous one. However, you shall visit the different countries with Jules Galdea as your escort, and be accorded every courtesy and kindness. Whenever you are ready to attempt a return voyage, I assure you that your boat which is here on exhibition shall be put in the waters of the river Heddekel at its mouth, and we will bid you Jehovah-speed."

Thus terminated our only interview with the High Priest or Ruler of the continent.

"There must have been five hundred of these thunder-throated monsters."

Part Four
In the Under World

WE learned that the males do not marry before they are from seventy-five to one hundred years old, and that the age at which women enter wedlock is only a little less, and that both men and women frequently live to be from six to eight hundred years old, and in some instances much older.

Josephus says: "God prolonged the life of the patriarchs that preceded the deluge, both on account of their virtues and to give them the opportunity of perfecting the sciences of geometry and astronomy, which they had discovered; which they could not have done if they had not lived 600 years, because it is only after the lapse of 600 years that the great year is accomplished."
–Flammarion, Astronomical Myths, Paris p. 26.

During the following year we visited many villages and towns, prominent among them being the cities of Nigi, Delft, Hectea, and my father was called upon no less than a half-dozen times to go over the maps which had been made from the rough sketches he had originally given of the divisions of land and water on the "outside" surface of the earth.

I remember hearing my father remark that the giant race of people in the land of "The Smoky God" had almost as accurate an idea of the geography of the "outside" surface of the earth as had the average college professor in Stockholm.

In our travels we came to a forest of gigantic trees, near the city of Delft. Had the Bible said there were trees towering over three hundred feet in height, and more than thirty feet in diameter, growing in the Garden Of Eden, the Ingersolls, the Tom Paines and Voltaires would doubtless have pronounced the statement a myth. Yet this is the description of the California sequoia gigantea; but these California giants pale into insignificance when compared with the forest Goliaths found in the "within" continent, where abound mighty trees from eight hundred to one thousand feet in height, and from one hundred to one hundred and twenty feet in diameter; countless in numbers and forming forests extending hundreds of miles back from the sea.

The people are exceedingly musical, and learned to a remarkable degree in their arts and sciences, especially geometry and astronomy. Their cities are equipped with vast palaces of music, where not infrequently as many as twenty-five thousand lusty voices of this giant race swell forth in mighty choruses of the most sublime symphonies.

The children are not supposed to attend institutions of learning before they are twenty years old. Then their school life begins and continues for thirty years, ten of which are uniformly devoted by both sexes to the study of music.

Their principal vocations are architecture, agriculture, horticulture, the raising of vast herds of cattle, and the building of conveyances peculiar to that country, for travel on land and water. By some device which I cannot explain, they hold communion with one another between the most distant parts of their country, on air currents.

All buildings are erected with special regard to strength, durability, beauty and symmetry, and with a style of architecture vastly more attractive to the eye than any I have ever observed elsewhere.

About three-fourths of the "inner" surface of the earth is land and about one-fourth water. There are numerous rivers of tremendous size, some flowing in a northerly direction and others southerly. Some of these rivers are thirty miles in width, and it is out of these vast waterways, at the extreme northern and southern parts of the "inside" surface of the earth, in regions where low temperatures are experienced, that freshwater icebergs are formed. They are then pushed out to sea like huge tongues of ice, by the abnormal freshets of turbulent waters that, twice every year, sweep everything before them.

We saw innumerable specimens of bird-life no larger than those encountered in the forests of Europe or America. It is well known that during the last few years whole species of birds have quit the earth. A writer in a recent article on this subject says:

Is it not possible that these disappearing bird species quit their habitation without, and find an asylum in the "within world"?

Whether inland among the mountains, or along the seashore, we found bird life prolific. When they spread their great wings some of the birds appeared to measure thirty feet from tip to tip. They are of great variety and many colors. We were permitted to climb up on the edge of a rock and examine a nest of eggs. There were five in the nest, each of which was at least two feet in length and fifteen inches in diameter.

Almost every year sees the final extinction of one or more bird species. Out of fourteen varieties of birds found a century since on a single island–the West Indian island of St. Thomas–eight have now to be numbered among the missing.

After we had been in the city of Hectea about a week, Professor Galdea took us to an inlet, where we saw thousands of tortoises along the sandy shore. I hesitate to state the size of these great creatures. They were from twenty-five to thirty feet in length, from fifteen to twenty feet in width and fully seven feet in height. When one of them projected its head it had the appearance of some hideous sea monster.

The strange conditions "within" are favorable not only for vast meadows of luxuriant grasses, forests of giant trees, and all manner of vegetable life, but wonderful animal life as well.

One day we saw a great herd of elephants. There must have been five hundred of these thunder-throated monsters, with their restlessly waving trunks. They were tearing huge boughs from the trees and trampling smaller growth into dust like so much hazel-brush. They would average over 100 feet in length and from 75 to 85 in height.

It seemed, as I gazed upon this wonderful herd of giant elephants, that I was again living in the public library at Stockholm, where I had spent much time studying the wonders of the Miocene age. I was filled with mute astonishment, and my father was speechless with awe. He held my arm with a protecting grip, as if fearful harm would overtake us. We were two atoms in this great forest, and, fortunately, unobserved by this vast herd of elephants as they drifted on and away, following a leader as does a herd of sheep. They browsed from growing herbage which they encountered as they traveled, and now and again shook the firmament with their deep bellowing.

"Moreover, there were a great number of elephants in the island: and there was provision for animals of every kind. Also whatever fragrant things there are in the earth., whether roots or herbage, or woods, or distilling drops of flowers or fruits, grew and thrived in that land."–The Cratyluo of Plato

There is a hazy mist that goes up from the land each evening, and it invariably rains once every twenty-four hours. This great moisture and the invigorating electrical light and warmth account perhaps for the luxuriant vegetation, while the highly charged electrical air and the evenness of climatic conditions may have much to do with the giant growth and longevity of all animal life.

In places the level valleys stretched away for many miles in every direction. "The Smoky God," in its clear white light, looked calmly down. There was an intoxication in the electrically surcharged air that fanned the cheek as softly as a vanishing whisper. Nature chanted a lullaby in the faint murmur of winds whose breath was sweet with the fragrance of bud and blossom.

After having spent considerably more than a year in visiting several of the many cities of the "within" world and a great deal of intervening country, and more than two years had passed from the time we had been picked up by the great excursion ship on the river, we decided to cast our fortunes once more upon the sea, and endeavor to regain the "outside" surface of the earth.

We made known our wishes, and they were reluctantly but promptly followed. Our hosts gave my father, at his request, various maps showing the entire "inside" surface of the earth, its cities, oceans, seas, rivers, gulfs and bays. They also generously offered to give us all the bags of gold nuggets–some of them as large as a goose's

61

egg–that we were willing to attempt to take with us in our little fishing-boat.

In due time we returned to Jehu, at which place we spent one month in fixing up and overhauling our little fishing sloop. After all was in readiness, the same ship "Naz" that originally discovered us, took us on board and sailed to the mouth of the river Hiddekel.

After our giant brothers had launched our little craft for us, they were most cordially regretful at parting, and evinced much solicitude for our safety. My father swore by the Gods Odin and Thor that he would surely return again within a year or two and pay them another visit. And thus we bade them adieu. We made ready and hoisted our sail, but there was little breeze. We were becalmed within an hour after our giant friends had left us and started on their return trip.

The winds were constantly blowing south, that is, they were blowing from the northern opening of the earth toward that which we knew to be south, but which, according to our compass's pointing finger, was directly north.

For three days we tried to sail, and to beat against the wind, but to no avail. Whereupon my father said: "My son, to return by the same route as we came in is impossible at this time of year. I wonder why we did not think of this before. We have been here almost two and a half years; therefore, this is the season when the sun is beginning to shine at the southern opening of the earth. The long cold night is on in the Spitzbergen country."

"What shall we do?" I inquired. "There is only one thing we can do," my father replied, "and that is to go south." Accordingly, he turned the craft about, gave it full reef, and sailed by the compass north but, in fact, directly south. The wind was strong, and we seemed to

have struck a current that was running with remarkable swiftness in the same direction.

In just forty days we arrived at Delft, a city we had
visited in company with our guides Jules Galdea and
his wife, near the mouth of the Gihon river. Here we
stopped for two days, and were most hospitably entertained by the same people who had welcomed us on
our former visit. We laid in some additional provisions
and again set sail, following the needle due north.

On our outward trip we came through a narrow
channel which appeared to be a separating body of
water between two considerable bodies of land. There
was a beautiful beach to our right, and we decided to
reconnoiter. Casting anchor, we waded ashore to rest
up for a day before continuing the outward hazardous
undertaking. We built a fire and threw on some sticks of
dry driftwood. While my father was walking along the
shore, I prepared a tempting repast from supplies we
had provided.

There was a mild, luminous light which my father
said resulted from the sun shining in from the south
aperture of the earth. That night we slept soundly, and
awakened the next morning as refreshed as if we had
been in our own beds at Stockholm.

After breakfast we started out on an inland tour of
discovery, but had not gone far when we sighted some
birds which we recognized at once as belonging to
the penguin family. They are flightless birds, but excellent swimmers and tremendous in size, with white
breast, short wings, black head, and long peaked bills.
They stand fully nine feet high. They looked at us with
little surprise, and presently waddled, rather than
walked, toward the water, and swam away in a northerly direction.

The events that occurred during the following hundred or more days beggar description. We were on an open and iceless sea. The month we reckoned to be November or December, and we knew the so-called South Pole was turned toward the sun. Therefore, when passing out and away from the internal electrical light of "The Smoky God" and its genial warmth, we would be met by the light and warmth of the sun, shining in through the south opening of the earth. We were not mistaken.

"The nights are never so dark at the Poles as in other regions, for the moon and stars seem to possess twice as much light and effulgence. In addition, there is a continuous light, the varied shades and play of which are amongst the strangest phenomena of nature."–Rambrosson's Astronomy.

There were times when our little craft, driven by wind that was continuous and persistent, shot through the waters like an arrow. Indeed, had we encountered a hidden rock obstacle, our little vessel would have been crushed into kindling-wood.

"The fact that gives the phenomenon of the polar aurora its greatest importance is that the earth becomes self-luminous; that, besides the light which as a planet is received from the central body, it shows a capability of sustaining a luminous process proper to itself."–Humboldt.

At last we were conscious that the atmosphere was growing decidedly colder, and, a few days later, icebergs were sighted far to the left. My father argued, and correctly, that the winds which filled our sails came from the warm climate "within." The time of the year was certainly most auspicious for us to make our dash for the "outside" world and attempt to scud our fishing sloop through open channels of the frozen zone which surrounds the polar regions.

We were soon amid the ice-packs, and how our little craft got through the narrow channels and escaped being crushed I know not. The coral pass behaved in the same drunken and unreliable fashion in passing over the southern curve or edge of the earth's shell as it had done on our inbound trip at the northern entrance. It gyrated, dipped and seemed like a thing possessed.

Captain Sabine, on page 105 in "Voyages in the Arctic Regions," says: "The geographical determination of the direction and intensity of the magnetic forces at different points of the earth's surface has been regarded as an object worthy of especial research. To examine in different parts of the globe, the declination, inclination and intensity of the magnetic force, and their periodical and secular variations, and mutual relations and dependencies could be duly investigated only in fixed magnetical observatories."

One day as I was lazily looking over the sloop's side into the clear waters, my father shouted: "Breakers ahead!" Looking up, I saw through a lifting mist a white object that towered several hundred feet high, completely shutting off our advance. We lowered sail immediately, and none too soon. In a moment we found ourselves wedged between two monstrous icebergs. Each was crowding and grinding against its fellow mountain of ice. They were like two gods of war contending for supremacy. We were greatly alarmed. Indeed, we were between the lines of a battle royal; the sonorous thunder of the grinding ice was like the continued volleys of artillery. Blocks of ice larger than a house were frequently lifted up a hundred feet by the mighty force of lateral pressure; they would shudder and rock to and fro for a few seconds, then come crashing down with a deafening roar, and disappear in the foaming waters. Thus, for more than two hours, the

"My father shouted, 'Breakers ahead!'"

contest of the ice giants continued.

It seemed as if the end had come. The ice pressure was terrific, and while we were not caught in the dangerous part of the jam, and were safe for the time being, yet the heaving and rending of tons of ice as it fell splashing here and there into the watery depths filled us with shaking fear.

Finally, to our great joy, the grinding of the ice ceased, and within a few hours the great mass slowly divided, and, as if an act of Providence had been performed, right before us lay an open channel. Should we venture with our little craft into this opening? If the pressure came on again, our little sloop as well as ourselves would be crushed into nothingness. We decided to take the chance, and, accordingly, hoisted our sail to a favoring breeze, and soon started out like a race-horse, running the gauntlet of this unknown narrow channel of open water.

"Less than a half mile away was a whaling vessel."

Part Five
Among the Ice Packs

FOR the next forty-five days our time was employed in dodging icebergs and hunting channels; indeed, had we not been favored with a strong south wind and a small boat, I doubt if this story could have ever been given to the world.

At last, there came a morning when my father said: "My son, I think we are to see home. We are almost through the ice. See! the open water lies before us."

However, there were a few icebergs that had floated far northward into the open water still ahead of us on either side, stretching away for many miles. Directly in front of us, and by the compass, which had now righted itself, due north, there was an open sea.

"What a wonderful story we have to tell to the people of Stockholm," continued my father, while a look of pardonable elation lighted up his honest face. "And think of the gold nuggets stowed away in the hold!"

I spoke kind words of praise to my father, not alone for his fortitude and endurance, but also for his courageous daring as a discoverer, and for having made the voyage that now promised a successful end. I was grateful, too, that he had gathered the wealth of gold we were carrying home.

While congratulating ourselves on the goodly supply of provisions and water we still had on hand, and on the dangers we had escaped, we were startled by hearing a most terrific explosion, caused by the tearing apart of a huge mountain of ice. It was a deafening roar like the firing of a thousand cannons. We were sailing at the time with great speed, and happened to be near a monstrous iceberg which to all appearances was as immovable as a rockbound island. It seemed, however, that the iceberg had split and was breaking apart, whereupon the balance of the monster which we were sailing was destroyed, and it began dipping from us. My father quickly anticipated the danger before I realized its awful possibilities. The iceberg extended down into the water many hundreds of feet, and, as it tipped over, the portion coming up out of the water caught our fishing-craft like a lever on a fulcrum, and threw it into the air as if it had been a football.

Our boat fell back on the iceberg that by this time had changed the side next to us for the top. My father was still in the boat, having become entangled in the rigging, while l was thrown some twenty feet away.

I quickly scrambled to my feet and shouted to my father, who answered: "All is well." Just then a realization dawned upon me. Horror upon horror! The blood froze in my veins. The iceberg was still in motion, and its great weight and force in toppling over would cause it to submerge temporarily. I fully realized what a sucking maelstrom it would produce amid the worlds of water on every side. They would rush into the depression in all their fury, like white-tangled wolves eager for human prey.

In this supreme moment of mental anguish, I remember glancing at our boat, which was lying on its side, and wondering if it could possibly right itself, and if my father could escape. Was this the end of our struggles and adventures? Was this death? All these questions flashed through my mind in the fraction of a second, and a moment later I was engaged in a life and death struggle. The ponderous monolith of ice sank below the surface, and the frigid waters gurgled around me in frenzied anger. I was in a saucer, with the waters pouring in on every side. A moment more and I lost consciousness.

When I partially recovered my senses, and roused from the swoon of a half-drowned man, I found myself wet, stiff, and almost frozen, lying on the iceberg. But there was no sign of my father or of our little fishing sloop. The monster berg had recovered itself, and, with its new balance, lifted its head perhaps fifty feet above the waves. The top of this island of ice was a plateau perhaps half an acre in extent.

I loved my father well, and was grief-stricken at the awfulness of his death. I railed at fate, that I, too, had not been permitted to sleep with him in the depths of the ocean. Finally, I climbed to my feet and looked about me. The purple-domed sky above, the shoreless green ocean beneath, and only an occasional iceberg discernible! My heart sank in hopeless despair. I cautiously picked my way across the berg toward the other side, hoping that our fishing craft had righted itself.

Dared I think it possible that my father still lived? It was but a ray of hope that flamed up in my heart. But the anticipation warmed my blood in my veins and started it rushing like some rare stimulant through every fiber of my body.

I crept close to the precipitous side of the iceberg, and peered far down, hoping, still hoping. Then I made a circle of the berg, scanning every foot of the way, and thus I kept going around and around. One part of my brain was certainly becoming maniacal, while the

71

other part, I believe, and do to this day, was perfectly rational.

I was conscious of having made the circuit a dozen times, and while one part of my intelligence knew, in all reason, there was not a vestige of hope, yet some strange fascinating aberration bewitched and compelled me still to beguile myself with expectation. The other part of my brain seemed to tell me that while there was no possibility of my father being alive, yet, if I quit making the circuitous pilgrimage, if I paused for a single moment, it would be acknowledgement of defeat, and, should I do this, I felt that I should go mad. Thus, hour after hour I walked around and around, afraid to stop and rest, yet physically powerless to continue much longer. Oh! horror of horrors! to be cast away on this wide expanse of waters without food or drink, and only a treacherous iceberg for an abiding place. My heart sank within me, and all semblance of hope was fading into black despair.

Then the hand of the Deliverer was extended, and the death-like stillness of a solitude rapidly becoming unbearable was suddenly broken by the firing of a signal-gun. I looked up in startled amazement, when, I saw, less than a half-mile away, a whaling vessel bearing down toward me with sail full set.

Evidently my continued activity on the iceberg had attracted their attention. On drawing near, they put out a boat, and, descending cautiously to the water's edge, I was rescued, and a little later lifted on board the whaling-ship.

I found it was a Scotch whaler, "The Arlington." She had cleared from Dundee in September, and started immediately for the Antarctic, in search of whales. The captain, Angus MacPherson, seemed kindly disposed, but in matters of discipline, as I soon learned, pos-

"Whereupon, I was put in irons."

sessed of an iron will. When I attempted to tell him that I had come from the "inside" of the earth, the captain and mate looked at each other, shook their heads, and insisted on my being put in a bunk under strict surveillance of the ship's physician.

I was very weak for want of food, and had not slept for many hours. However, after a few days rest, I got up one morning and dressed myself without asking permission of the physician or anyone else, and told them that I was as sane as anyone.

The captain sent for me and again questioned me concerning where I had come from and how I came to be alone on an iceberg in the far off Antarctic Ocean. I replied that I had just come from the "inside" of the earth, and proceeded to tell him how my father and myself had gone in by Spitzbergen, and came out by way of the South Pole country, whereupon I was put in irons. I afterward heard the captain tell the mate that I was as crazy as a March hare, and that I must remain in confinement until I was rational enough to give a truthful account of myself.

Finally, after much pleading and many promises, I was released from irons. I then and there decided to invent some story that would satisfy the captain, and never again refer to my trip to the land of "The Smoky God," at least until I was safe among friends.

Within a fortnight, I was permitted to go about and take my place as one of the seamen. A little later the captain asked me for an explanation. I told him that my experience had been so horrible that I was fearful of my memory, and begged him to permit me to leave the question unanswered until some time in the future. "I think you are recovering considerably," he said, "but you are not sane yet by a good deal." "Permit me to do such work as you may assign," I replied, "and if it does

74

not compensate you sufficiently, I will pay you immediately after I reach Stockholm–to the last penny." Thus the matter rested.

On finally reaching Stockholm, as I have already related, I found that my good mother had gone to her reward more than a year before. I have also told how, later, the treachery of a relative landed me in a madhouse, where I remained for twenty-eight years–seemingly unending years–and, still later, after my release, how I returned to the life of a fisherman, following it sedulously for twenty-seven years, then how I came to America and finally to Los Angeles, California. But all this can be of little interest to the reader. Indeed, it seems to me the climax of my wonderful travels and strange adventures was reached when the Scotch sailing-vessel took me from an iceberg on the Antarctic Ocean.

Part Six
Conclusion

In concluding this history of my adventures, I wish to state that I firmly believe science is yet in its infancy concerning the cosmology of the earth. There is so much that is unaccounted for by the world's accepted knowledge of to-day, and will ever remain so until the land of "The Smoky God" is known and recognized by our geographers.

It is the land from whence came the great logs of cedar that have been found by explorers in the open waters far over the northern edge of the earth's crust, and also the bodies of mammoths whose bones are found in vast beds on the Siberian coast.

Northern explorers have done much. Sir John Franklin, De Haven Grinnell, Sir John Murray, Kane, Melville, Hall, Nansen, Schwatka, Greely, Peary, Ross, Gerlache, Bernacchi, Andree, Amsden, Amundson and others have all been striving to storm the frozen citadel of mystery.

I firmly believe that Andree and his two brave companions, Strindberg and Fraenckell, who sailed away in the balloon "Oreon" from the northwest coast of Spitzbergen on that Sunday afternoon of July 11, 1897, are now in the "within" world, and doubtless are being entertained, as my father and myself were entertained by the kind-hearted giant race inhabiting the inner Atlantic Continent.

Having, in my humble way, devoted years to these problems, I am well acquainted with the accepted definitions of gravity, as well as the cause of the magnetic needle's attraction, and I am prepared to say that it is my firm belief that the magnetic needle is influenced solely by electric currents which completely envelope the earth like a garment. and that these electric currents in an endless circuit pass out of the southern end of the earth's cylindrical opening, diffusing and spreading themselves over all of the "outside" surface, and rushing madly on in their course toward the North Pole. And while these currents seemingly dash off into space at the earth's curve or edge, yet they drop again to the "inside" surface and continue their way southward along the inside of the earth's crust, toward the opening of the so-called South Pole.

As to gravity, no one knows what it is because it has not been determined whether it is atmospheric pressure that causes the apple to fall, or whether, 150 miles below the surface of the earth, supposedly one-half way through the earth's crust, there exists some powerful loadstone attraction that draws it. Therefore, whether the apple, when it leaves the limb of the tree, is drawn or impelled downward to the nearest point of resistance, is unknown to the students of physics.

"Mr. Lemstrom concluded that an electric discharge which could only be seen by means of the spectroscope was taking place on the surface of the ground all around him, and that from a distance it would appear as a faint display of Aurora, the phenomena of pale and flaming light which is sometimes seen on the top of the Spitzbergen Mountains."–The Arctic Manual, page 739.

Sir James Ross claimed to have discovered the magnetic pole at about seventy-four degrees latitude. This is wrong–the magnetic pole is exactly one-half the distance through the earth's crust. Thus, if the earth's crust is three hundred miles in thickness, which is the distance I estimate it to be, then the magnetic pole is undoubtedly one hundred and fifty miles below the surface of the earth, it matters not where the test is made. And at this particular point one hundred and fifty miles below the surface, gravity ceases, becomes neutralized; and when we pass beyond that point on toward the "inside" surface of the earth, a reverse attraction geometrically increases in power, until the other one hundred and fifty miles of distance is traversed, which would bring us out on the "inside" of the earth.

Thus, if a hole were bored down through the earth's crust at London, Paris, New York, Chicago, or Los Angeles, a distance of three hundred miles, it would connect the two surfaces. While the inertia and momentum of a weight dropped in from the "outside" surface would carry it far past the magnetic center, yet, before reaching the "inside" surface of the earth, it would gradually diminish in speed, after passing the halfway point, finally pause and immediately fall back toward the "outside" surface, like the swinging of a pendulum with the power removed, until it would finally rest at the magnetic center, or at that particular point exactly one-half the distance between the "outside" surface and the "inside" surface of the earth.

The gyration of the earth in its daily act of whirling around in its spiral rotation–at a rate greater than one thousand miles every hour, or about seventeen miles per second–makes of it a vast electrogenerating body, a huge machine, a mighty prototype of the puny-man-made dynamo, which, at best, is but a feeble imitation of nature's original.

The valleys of this inner Atlantis Continent, bordering the upper waters of the farthest north are in season covered with the most magnificent and luxuriant flowers. Not hundreds and thousands, but millions, of acres, from which the pollen or blossoms are carried far away in almost every direction by the earth's spiral gyrations and the agitation of the wind resulting therefrom, and it is these blossoms or pollen from the vast floral meadows "within" that produce the colored snows of the Arctic regions that have so mystified the northern explorers.

Beyond question, this new land "within" is the home, the cradle, of the human race, and viewed from the standpoint of the discoveries made by us, must of necessity have a most important bearing on all physical, paleontological, archeological, philological and mythological theories of antiquity.

Kane, vol. I, page 44, says: "We passed the 'crimson cliffs' of Sir John Ross in the forenoon of August 5th. The patches of red snow from which they derive their name could be seen clearly at the distance of ten miles from the coast."

La Chambre, in an account of Andree's balloon expedition, on page 144, says: "On the isle of Amsterdam, the snow is tinted with red for a considerable distance, and the savants are collecting it to examine it microscopically. It presents, in fact, certain peculiarities; it is thought that it contains very small planets. Scoreby, the famous whaler, had already remarked this."

The same idea of going back to the land of mystery-to the very beginning-to the origin of man–is found in Egyptian traditions of the earlier terrestrial regions of the gods, heroes and men from the historical fragments of Manetho, fully verified by the historical records taken from the more recent excavations of Pompeii as well as the traditions of the North American Indians.

It is now one hour past midnight –the new year of 1908 is here, and this is the third day thereof, and having at last finished the record of my strange travels and adventures I wish given to the world, I am ready, and even longing, for the peaceful rest which I am sure will follow life's trials and vicissitudes. I am old in years, and ripe both with adventures and sorrows, yet rich with the few friends I have cemented to me in my struggles to lead a just and upright life. Like a story that is well-nigh told, my life is ebbing away. The presentiment is strong within me that I shall not live to see the rising of another sun. Thus do I conclude my message.

OLAF JENSEN

Part Seven
Author's Afterword

I FOUND much difficulty in deciphering and editing the manuscripts of Olaf Jansen. However, I have taken the liberty of reconstructing only a very few expressions, and in doing this have in no way changed the spirit or meaning. Otherwise, the original text has neither been added to nor taken from.

It is impossible for me to express my opinion as to the value of reliability of the wonderful statements made by Olaf Jansen. The description here given of the strange lands and people visited by him, location of cities, the names and directions of rivers, and other information herein combined, conform in every way to the rough drawings given into my custody by this ancient Norseman, which drawings together with the manuscript it is my intention at some later date to give to the Smithsonian Institution, to preserve for the benefit of those interested in the mysteries of the "Farthest North"–the frozen circle of silence. It is certain there are many things in Vedic literature, in "Josephus," the "Odyssey," the "Iliad," Terrien de Lacouperie's "Early History of Chinese Civilization," Flammarion's "Astronomical Myths," Lenormant's "Beginnings of History," Hesoid's "Theogony," Sir John de Maundeville's writings, and Sayce's "Records of the Past," that, to say the

least, are strangely in harmony with the seemingly
incredible text found in the yellow manuscript of the
old Norseman, Olaf Jansen, and now for the first time
given to the world.

WILLIS GEORGE EMERSON

The "Inner Earth" theory got a tremendous shot in the arm when publisher Ray Palmer released this issue of his privately-published *Flying Saucers* magazine in December, 1959.

Part Eight
Saucers From Earth!

Introduction

THE LATE Ray Palmer started writing science-fiction in the 1930s, and later became editor of *Amazing Stories* and other science-fiction magazines in the 1940s. He soon shocked the world when he published the "true tales" of one reader–Richard Shaver–who maintained that he was in contact with beings from the depth of the Earth.

Later on, as editor of his own magazine–*Flying Saucers*–Palmer shocked the sensibilities of his readers when he proclaimed, in the December, 1959 issue, that the Earth was hollow and could be entered at either the North or South Pole. This is a direct reprint of the astounding revelations he brought to the public.

• • •

A Challenge to Secrecy!

Flying Saucers has amassed a large file of evidence which its editors consider unassailable, to prove that the flying saucers are native to the planet Earth; that the governments of more than one nation (if not all of them) know this to be fact; that a concerted effort is being made to learn all about them, and to explore their native land; that the facts already known are considered so important that they are the world's top secret; that the danger is so great that to offer public proof is to risk widespread panic; that public knowledge would bring public demand for action which would topple governments both helpless and unwilling to comply; that the inherent nature of the flying saucers and their origination area is completely disruptive to political and economic status-quo.

Since the day Kenneth Arnold first brought flying saucers to wide public attention by his famous sighting, one fact has been consistently brought forth by investigator-flying saucers did not originate with that sighting, but have been with humanity for centuries if not thousands of years. Flying Saucers is the popular term for Unidentified Flying Objects (UFO), or Unidentified Aerial Phenomena (UAP). The popular "saucer" shape is only a segment of the phenomena. Properly, the important fact to consider is that intelligently controlled phenomena appear in our atmosphere. Their exact nature is a matter for conjecture, and is quite varied in configuration (to use a favorite Air Force word). It is this fact of antiquity which poses the most important single factor in analyzing the phenomena. At one stroke it eliminates contemporary earth governments as the originators of the mysterious phenomena.

Because of this antiquity, many investigators have turned from the earth to other planets, and to other solar systems. Each planet has its followers in this group of investigators, and such bodies as Venus, Mars and Saturn are favorites with the so-called contactees. We are not at all concerned in this symposium of evidence with the contactee—a phenomenon as "unidentified" as UFO themselves. It may not even be remotely related. However, chief among the advocates of inter-planetary origin is Major Donald E. Keyhoe, whose efforts are entirely directed toward collecting evidence that will serve to advance this theory. The interplanetary theorist has a large following, and is perhaps the only theory that will even be considered by scientific men such as astronomers. While it is true that there are many mysteries of an interplanetary nature, linking them with UFO demands a stretching of the evidence, and a great deal of extrapolation. It may be true that there are "configurations" on the Moon, for instance, which are used by Keyhoe to postulate "flying saucers" on that body. Unfortunately (for Keyhoe) this same evidence is used by contactees such as Adamski to support their contentions. Actually, the Moon is remote, in reference to Unidentified Aerial Phenomena, and we must disregard it when we speak of atmospheric phenomena: events which occur within our atmosphere. Since almost all "sightings" are in the atmosphere in nature, the greatest percentage of thinking on them must be limited to the atmosphere.

Because our planet is quite well (but not completely) known, it has been easy for interplanetary theorists to prove that the strange objects are not made by any single government or group of governments on Earth. Such a vast project could not remain secret over so long a period, and also, the matter of antiquity does not allow the phenomena to be fitted into the history of existing governments.

How well-known is the Earth? Is there any area on Earth which can be regarded as a possible origin for the flying saucers? There are two, speaking in major terms, and four, speaking in more minor terminology. The two major areas, in order of importance, are Antarctica and the Arctic. The South Polar continent, and the North Polar area. We speak of the North Polar area because exploration made public to date indicates there is no land, but that it is an ocean, frozen over with ice, under which exploration by submarine is being carried on. The two minor areas are South America's Matto Grosso and Asia's Tibetan Highlands.

Could the flying saucers come from any of these areas? We can largely eliminate the Matto Grosso and the Tibetan Highlands; firstly because of the enormous numbers of the UFO, and secondly because these areas are not entirely unexplored, and can be flown over almost at will. Evidence is lacking in both these areas. Negative evidence, however, does exist in some measure, sufficiently to cause theorists to discard both areas, except in a minor way. At most, either or both Matto Grosso and Tibetan Highland, can be suspected to be "bases" or something on the order of "way stations".

What about the North Pole? Explorers say it is entirely oceanic in nature, covered with ice which sometimes melts in part, and in many areas is quite thin at all times. The depth of the ocean beneath this ice varies from some 24 fathoms to several miles. Flights have been made to and across the North Pole. Submarines, notably *Nautilus* and *Skate*, have traveled to the Pole and returned, crossing from one side to the other (Point Barrow to Spitzbergen). Apparently the sort of base necessary for the UFO mystery in its entirety does not exist in the North Polar regions.

What about the South Pole? Here we have a continent quite as large as North and South America combined, insofar as land mass is concerned. At least one large area (40,000 square miles) is known to experience 100% melting during the summer, and even in winter possesses warm water lakes (from warm springs, geysers, etc). This area is under control of the Russians, who have a permanent base there. Expeditions from both Little America and from the British zone of exploration, have reached the South Pole. Expeditions have also reached the South Magnetic Pole. This is a distinction it is necessary to stress, due to the strange fact that the South Magnetic Pole is actually 2300 miles distant from the South Geographic Pole. It is a fact that a tremendous land area exists in the South Pole Continental Area which is unexplored and which constitutes a large blank on the map of the Earth.

Let us consider the North Pole first, and discover what we know about it. What are the facts about the "top" of the Earth?

First, it is surrounded on all sides by known areas of land. Siberia, Spitzbergen, Alaska, Canada, Finland, Norway, Greenland, Iceland. The northern shores of these lands border on the Arctic Ocean, in the virtual center of which both the geographic and magnetic poles exist. These two poles are separated by less than 200 miles, and one of them, the magnetic pole, is known to "wander" somewhat.

The North Pole has been reached by a number of expeditions. The latest we know of are the exploits of the *Nautilus* and *Skate,* both atomic submarines which traversed the entire extent of the Arctic Ocean beneath the ice, making the Pole itself (magnetic) a stopping point. On the surface of things, it can be said that the North Polar Area is fairly well explored. In addition to our submarine explorations, the Russians have also traversed the Arctic Ocean. They have even established magnetic "bases", navigational aids which they have planted along Alaskan and Canadian shores, so that rocket-launching atomic bomb submarines can proceed swiftly to a prearranged launching site, and fire rockets on prearranged courses. American submarines

88

have been busily (we hope) moving these navigational aids to new sites which throw off the prearranged calculations, thus making them worthless.

But there is an area of doubt which *Flying Saucers* intends to explore, and to present as the first of its bits of evidence which point to what may well be the best-kept secret in history. In order to do so, we must go back to 1947. In February of that year, Admiral Richard E. Byrd, the one man who has done the most to make the North Pole a known area, made the following statement: "I'd like to see that land beyond the Pole. That area beyond the Pole is the center of the great Unknown."

Millions of people read his statement in their daily newspapers. And millions thrilled to the Admiral's subsequent flight to the Pole and to a point 1700 miles beyond it. Millions heard the radio broadcast description of that flight, which was also published in the newspapers. Briefly, for the benefit of our readers, we will recount that flight as it progressed. When the plane took off from its Arctic base, it proceeded straight north to the Pole. From that point, it flew on a total of 1700 miles beyond the Pole, and then retraced its course to its Arctic base. As progress was made beyond the Pole point, iceless land and lakes, mountains covered with trees, and even a monstrous animal moving through the underbrush, were observed and reported via radio by the plane's occupants. For almost all of the 1700 miles the plane flew over land, mountains, trees, lakes, rivers.

What land was it? Look at your map. Calculate the distance to the Pole from all the known lands we have previously mentioned. A good portion of them are well within the 1700 mile range. But none of them are within 200 miles of the Pole Byrd flew over no known land. He himself called it "the great unknown." And great it is, indeed! For after 1700 miles over land, he was forced by gasoline supply limit to return, and he had not yet reached the end of it! He should have been well inside one of the known areas mentioned. He should have been back to "civilization". But he was not. He should have seen nothing but ice-covered ocean, or at the very most, partially open ocean. Instead he was over mountains covered with forests.

Forests!

Incredible! The northernmost limit of the timberline is located well down into Alaska, Canada and Siberia. North of that line no tree grows! All around the North Pole, the tree does not grow within 1700 miles of the Pole!

What have we here? We have the well-authenticated flight of Admiral Richard E. Byrd to a land beyond the Pole that he so much wanted to see, because it was the center of the unknown, the center of mystery. Apparently he had his wish gratified to the fullest, yet today, in 1959, nowhere is that mysterious land mentioned. Why? Was that 1947 flight fiction? Did all the newspapers lie? Did the radio from Byrd's plane lie?

No, Admiral Byrd did fly beyond the Pole.

Beyond?

What did the Admiral mean when he used that word? How is it possible to go "beyond" the Pole? Let us consider for a moment: Let us imagine that we are transported, by some miraculous means, to the exact point of the North Magnetic Pole. We arrive there instantaneously, not knowing from which direction we came. And all we know is that we are to proceed from the Pole to Spitzbergen. But where is Spitzbergen? Which way do we go? South, of course! But which south? All directions from the North Pole are south!

This is actually a simple navigational problem. All

expeditions to the Pole, whether flown, or by submarine, or on foot, have been faced with this problem. Either they must retrace their steps, or discover which southerly direction is the correct one to their destination, whatever it has been determined to be. The problem is solved by making a turn, in *any* direction, and proceeding approximately 20 miles. Then we stop, shoot the stars, correlate with our compass reading (which no longer points straight down, but toward the North Magnetic Pole), and plot our course on the map. Then it is a simple matter to proceed to Spitzbergen by going south.

Admiral Byrd did not follow this traditional navigational procedure: when he reached the Pole, he *continued on* for 1700 miles. To all intents and purposes, he continued on a northerly course, after crossing the Pole. And weirdly, it stands on the record that he succeeded, for he did see that "land beyond the Pole" which to this day, if we are to scan the records of newspapers, book, radio, television and word of mouth, has never been revisited!

That land, on today's maps, *cannot exist.* But since it *does,* we can only conclude that today's maps are incorrect, incomplete, and do not present a true picture of the northern hemisphere!

Having thus located a great land mass in the North, not on any map today, a land which *is* the *center of the great unknown,* which can only be construed to imply that the 1700 mile extent traversed by Byrd is only *a portion* of it, let us go to the South Pole and see what we can learn about it.

On April 5, 1955, the U.S. Navy announced an expedition to the South Pole. It was to be headed by Admiral Richard E. Byrd. It consisted of five ships, fourteen airplanes, special tractors, and a complement of

The central sun as it would appear to an explorer when he had reached the spot indicated by the letter "D" on the diagram, if the atmospheric conditions were favorable.

1393 men. The stated purpose of the expedition was as follows: "To construct a satellite base at the South Pole."

In San Francisco, on the eve of his departure, Admiral Byrd delivered a radio address in which he stated: "This is the most important expedition in the history of the world."

Let us pause a moment and pretend we are rocket men, primarily the scientist-rocket-men who are engaged in launching satellites. Our task is a troublesome one. Many failures result. Our work is a tremendously difficult task, and sometimes important rocket shoots are delayed for days by weather. Our base is a gigantic one, here at Cape Canaveral. The logistics problem is enormous. The rockets themselves weigh hundreds of tons. To be asked to set up such a satellite base at the South Pole would cause us to stare in utter amazement at the official making the request. We would waste no time in informing him that he hasten immediately to his psychiatrist and retire from active service, for he has indeed "gone off his rocker". In short, a satellite base at the tip of South America in plain words, is totally ridiculous. Even a satellite tracking station at the South Pole is nothing short of idiotic. For tracking purposes, a base at the tip of South America is entirely adequate. Or on a series of ships anchored about the Antarctic Circle.

This, then, cannot be a satellite base. It must be something else. On January 13, 1956, we learn what it really is. On that date the U.S. Navy flies to a point 2300 miles beyond the South Pole. The entire distance is accomplished over land.

Once again, look at your map. Unlike the North Polar Sea, the South Polar Continent is entirely surrounded by water. And in all cases, no matter what direction you proceed from the South Pole, you pass from the continental area to a known oceanic area. You proceed hundreds of miles over water to reach a distance of 2300 miles.

Once again we have penetrated an unknown and mysterious land which does not appear on today's maps. And once again, we find no further announcement beyond the initial announcement of the achievement.

And strangest of all, we find the world's millions absorbing the announcements, and registering a complete blank insofar as curiosity is concerned. Nobody, hearing the announcements, or reading of them in the newspaper, bothers to get a map and *check* the facts! Or if they do, they only shake their heads in puzzlement, and then shrug their shoulders. If Admiral Byrd is not bothered with the apparent inconsistencies, why should they be?

Here, then, are the *facts:* At *both* poles exist unknown and vast land areas, not in the least uninhabitable, extending for distances which can only be called tremendous, because they encompass an area bigger than any known continental area! The North Polar Mystery Land seen by Byrd and his crew is at least 1700 miles across its traversed direction, and cannot be conceived to be merely a narrow strip, as the factor of coincidence in flying precisely along its longest extent is improbable. It is a land area perhaps as large as the entire United States! The land area at the South Pole, considering that the flight began 400 miles west of the Pole, and thus covers a continuous land area of 2700 miles in *one* direction, means a land area possibly as big as North America *in addition* to the known extent of the South Polar Continent, which is located *north* of the Pole whereas the 2300-mile land traversed by the Navy plane is "beyond" the Pole. Once more the same condition of navigation exists: progress was made to the Pole and then *straight on beyond it,* with the one difference that the South Geographic Pole is located 2300 miles away from the South Magnetic Pole, and it is not necessary to perform the navigational maneuver described previously. If navigating from the South Magnetic Pole, the procedure is again necessary, with differences due to the greater angle of inclination to the stars, and the possibility of navigation entirely by the stars rather than with the aid of a compass.

Let's stop here and make a statement that logically follows: the flying saucers could come from these two unknown lands "beyond the Poles". It is the opinion of the editors of *Flying Saucers* that the existence of these lands cannot be disproved by anyone, considering. the facts of the two expeditions which we have outlined. These facts can be checked by anyone. You have merely to read the newspapers of the day. If there is anyone who can satisfactorily explain away these two expeditions, and the statements of Admiral Richard E. Byrd concerning them, *Flying Saucers* will give him every inch of space necessary to complete his explanation.

Just for the record, let's present the actual announcement carried by press and radio on February 5, 1956: "On January 13, members of the United States expedition accomplished a flight of 2700 miles from the base at McMurado Sound which is 400 miles west of the South Pole, and penetrated a land extent of 2300 miles beyond the Pole."

And on March 13, Admiral Byrd reported, upon his return from the South Pole: "The present expedition has opened up a vast new land."

Finally, in 1957, before his death, he reported it as: "That enchanted continent in the sky, land of everlasting mystery!" Which statement remains to your editors as the most mysterious of all, and almost inexplicable. "Enchanted continent in the sky..." Everlasting mystery, indeed!

Considering all this, is there any wonder that all the nations of the world have suddenly found the South Polar region (particularly), because of its known land area and the North Pole region so intensely interesting and important, and have launched explorations on a scale truly tremendous in scope?

And was it because of Admiral Byrd's weird flight into an unknown Polar land in 1947 that the International Geophysical Year was conceived in that year, and finally brought to fruition ten years later, and is actually, still going on? Did his flight make it suddenly imperative to discover the real nature of this planet we live on, and solve the tremendous mysteries that unexpectedly confronted us?

If you have followed us thus far, it may be that you have gone to your map or your globe and have tried to fit these mysterious lands onto the planet, and have come up with a snort and said: "These bits of evidence are all very well, but the fact remains there is nowhere physically to place these land masses. Since the space to do so is lacking, there exists a fundamental impossibility which cannot be overcome." Good boy! Don't give up your guns. Insist that we overcome this fundamental impossibility, and support our original evidence in not a few ways, but in hundreds....

The question that most logically follows the two instances of exploration which we have outlined is whether or not other Polar Expeditions have encountered similar and confirming conditions. In order to answer this question, it will be necessary to examine the records of all North and South Pole explorations from the very first of which modern man has any knowledge. As a sub-subject, it might be interesting later on to go into legend and mythology for still further bits of confirmation, but we are concerned now only with presenting provable facts. In the presentation of these facts, we intend to draw no conclusion. They should become obvious to the reader without prompting.

To those of our readers so inclined, there must be a great deal of interest on their part In the historically famous debate on which, or both, or neither, Cook or Perry actually reached the North Pole. In the years following these expeditions, much debate went on, and even today arguments rage. Briefly, let's outline the claims of both men.

Dr. Frederick A. Cook said he reached the Pole on April 21, 1908. His announcement was followed by a few days by one from Rear Admiral Robert E. Peary that he had reached the Pole on April 6, 1909. Both men hurled accusations against the other, Cook even saying that Peary had appropriated some of his stores cached against his return from the Pole. Cook in his turn failed to supply notes he said he had kept of his trip, and thereby cast doubt an his own story. The reader who is interested in the whole story should visit his library and read up on the controversy.

Although Cook claims to have been the first to reach the Pole we will take Peary's claim, which has been universally recognized, and examine it. Cook's claim was discredited on one basis because the sun's altitude was so low that observations of it as proof of position were worthless. It should be noted that Peary also reached the Pole in April, 15 days earlier in the season, and therefore under even more adverse solar observations conditions. His calculations therefore are more suspect than Cook's. Cook, it was said, had no witnesses other than Eskimos; the same is true of Peary. Peary, however, lacked witnesses through choice, having ordered his white companions to remain behind, while he went on alone with one Eskimo companion to the Pole. Cook was doubted in his claim that he averaged 15 miles a day. Peary claimed to have made over 20. Undoubtedly the argument will never be settled. However, there is the factor regarding Peary's dash to the Pole, which, in our opinion, is quite remarkable. This factor lies in the fantastic speed with which he made his trip.

When Peary neared the 88th parallel, he decided to attempt the final dash to the Pole in five days. He made 25 miles the first day; 20 on the second; 20 on the third; 25 on the fourth; 40 on the fifth. His five-day average was 26 miles. On the return trip he traveled a total of 153 miles in two days, including a halt 5 miles from the Pole to take a sounding of the ocean depth. This is an average of 76½ miles per day. His actual traveling time was approximately 19 hours per day. This is a *walking* speed of 4 miles per hour. Can a man walk that fast under the incredible conditions of the North Pole area, an ice-terrain described by the men of the atomic submarine Skate as fantastically jumbled and jagged? And yet, further south, with presumably better going, he was able to average only 20 miles per day.

We stress the distances only because the ones nearest the Pole are weirdly impossible. Only if Peary was reporting honestly would we have included such contradictory calculations which he must have known would discredit his story. Therefore we can assume that he did report honestly, and that we have a speed of travel which projects into the same mysterious area in the same "unfittable" manner as a whole vast continent fits into a space that is totally lacking. When traveling over a land whose dimensions are fantastically "expanded,' will we not also travel at an equally fantastically "expanded" speed? It will be well to remember

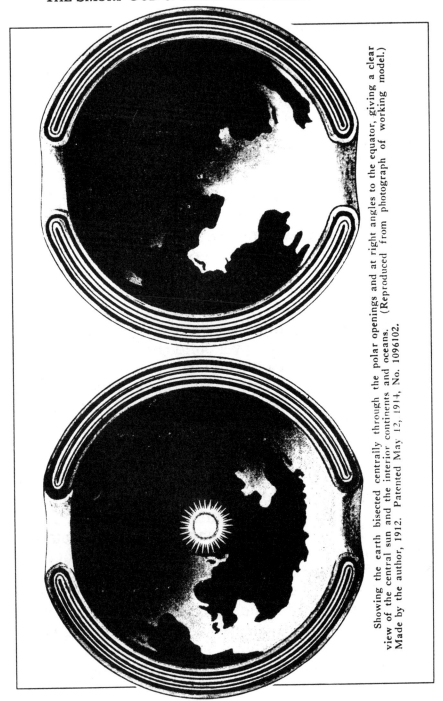

Showing the earth bisected centrally through the polar openings and at right angles to the equator, giving a clear view of the central sun and the interior continents and oceans. (Reproduced from photograph of working model.) Made by the author, 1912. Patented May 12, 1914, No. 1096102.

that these speeds were calculated by astronomical observation, because the astronomical basis of these calculations will be taken up later in presentation of evidence.

To those who will study up on the subject of Polar Exploration, it will soon become evident that the feature most agreed upon by all North Polar explorers is that the area is oceanic, covered by water, and that it is variously frozen over or partially open, depending on the time of year. One peculiarity which many explorers remark upon, however, is that paradoxically, the open water exists in greater measure at the nearer reaches of the Pole. In fact, some explorers found it very hot going at times, and were forced to shed their Arctic clothing; there even being one record of an encounter with naked Eskimos. Yet, with all this confirmed oceanic area, we have the contradiction of Admiral Byrd's flight being almost entirely over land, mountains covered with trees, interspersed with lakes and streams.

One of the reports from Byrd's expedition was the sighting of a huge animal with dark fur. Are there such animals, or traces of them, in the Arctic? Beginning in Siberia, along the Lena river, there lie exposed on the soil, and buried within it, the bones and tusks of literally millions of mammoths and mastodons. The consensus of scientific opinion is that these are prehistoric remains, and that the mammoth existed some 20,000 years ago, and was wiped out in the unknown catastrophe we now call the last Ice Age. In 1799, a fisherman named Schumachoff, living in Tongoose (Siberia), discovered a complete mammoth frozen in a clear block of ice. Hacking it free, he despoiled it of its huge tusks and left the carcass of fresh meat be be devoured by wolves. Later an expedition set out to examine it, and today its skeleton may still be seen in the Museum of

Natural History in Petrograd (then St. Petersburg).

Early in the century, approximately 1910, a very scientific meal was served in Petrograd. It consisted of wheat from the Egyptian tombs, preserved foods from Pompeii and Herculaneum, mammoth meat from Siberia, and other interesting and ancient viands. The mammoth meat was fresh, and the mammoth from which it had been taken still had undigested food in its stomach, this undigested food consisting of young shocks of fir and pine and young fir cones. According to the scientists, this mammoth was one of the millions slain instantly in a gigantic catastrophe 20,000 years ago, in a habitat then tropical, in which the vegetation was fern and tropical in nature. Yet, in the stomach of this mammoth is found the sparse food of a sub-Arctic area such as much of Alaska or Northern Canada is today. There is good reason to cast doubt upon the tropic origin of the mammoth, and its sudden demise. And if the demise was not sudden, then the presence of indigested food (not digested even by so much as minutes exposure to stomach acids) in the stomach of the mammoth is unexplainable. True the death must have been sudden, but it was not of tropic locale. If not tropic, then the Ice Age onset is not the cause of death. The cause of death, then, is Arctic in nature, and could have occurred any time. But since the Ice Age, there have been no mammoths in the known world. Unless they exist in the mysterious land beyond the Pole, where one of them was actually seen alive by members of the Byrd expedition! Others who dined on mammoth meat were James Oliver Curwood and Gabrielle D'Annunzio, who gave a banquet at the Hotel Carlton in Paris.

We have taken the mammoth as a rather sensational modern evidence of Byrd's mysterious land, but there are many lesser proofs that an unknown originating point exists somewhere in the northern reaches. We will merely list a few, suggesting that the reader, in examining the records of polar explorers for the past two centuries, will find evidences of both fauna and flora impossible to reconcile with the known areas of land mentioned early in this presentation of facts, those areas surrounding the Polar Area on your present-day maps.

The musk-ox, contrary to expectations, migrates north in the wintertime. Repeatedly, Arctic explorers have observed bear heading north into an area where there is no food for them. Foxes also are found north of the goth parallel, heading north, obviously well-fed. Without exception, Arctic explorers agree that the further north one goes, the warmer it gets. Invariably, a north wind brings warmer weather. Coniferous trees drift ashore, from out of the north. Butterflies and bees are found in the far north, but never hundreds miles further south; not until Canadian and Alaskan climate conducive to such insect life are reached. Unknown varieties of flowers are found. Birds resembling snipe, but unlike any known species of bird, come out of the north, and return there. Hare are plentiful in an area where no vegetation ever grows, but where vegetation appears as drifting debris from the northern open waters. Eskimo tribes, migrating northward, have left unmistakable traces of their migration in their temporary camps, always advancing northward. Southern Eskimos themselves speak of tribes that live in the far north. The Ross gull, common at Point Barrow, migrates in October toward the north. Only Admiral Byrd's "mystery land" can account for these inexplicable facts and migrations.

The Scandinavian legend of a wonderful land far to

the North called "Ultima Thule" (commonly confused today with Greenland) is significant when studied in detail, because of its remarkable resemblance to the kind of land seen by Byrd, and its remarkable far north location. To assume that Ultima Thule is Greenland is to come face to face with the contradiction of the Greenland Ice Cap, which fill the entire Greenland basin to a depth of 10,000 feet. A green, fertile land in this location places itself so deep in antiquity that it postulates an overturn of the Earth, and a new North Pole area (see National Geographic's exploration of the Greenland Ice Cap and its possible significance).

Is Admiral Byrd's land of mystery, center of the great unknown, the same as the Ultima Thule of the Scandinavian legends?

There are mysteries concerning the Antarctic also. Perhaps the greatest is a highly technical one of biology itself; for on the New Zealand and South American land masses are identical fauna and flora which could not have migrated from one to the other, but rather are believed to have come from a common motherland. That motherland is believed to be the Antarctic Continent. But on a more "popular" level is the case of the sailing vessel *Gladys* captained by E.B. Hatfield, in 1893. The ship was completely surrounded by icebergs at 43 degrees south and 33 degrees west and finally escaped its entrapment at 40 degrees south and 30 degrees west. At this latitude an iceberg was observed which bore a large quantity of sand and earth, and which revealed a beaten track, a place of refuge formed in a sheltered nook, and the bodies of five dead men who lay on different parts of the berg. Bad weather prevented any attempts at further investigation.

Bear in mind that it is a unanimous consensus of opinion among scientists that the one thing peculiar to the Antarctic is that there are no human tribes living upon it. But this consensus must be wrong, because investigation showed that no vessel was lost in the Antarctic at that time, so that these dead men could not have been shipwrecked sailors. Even today, with Antarctic exploration at its height, the lack of human life on that bleak continent is agreed upon. Could it be that these men who died on that berg came from "that mysterious land beyond the South Pole" discovered by the Byrd expedition? Had they ventured out of their warm, habitable land and lost their way along the ice shelf, finally to be drifted to their deaths at sea on a portion of it, broken away to become an iceberg while they were on it?

Most recent evidence that there is something strange about the Poles of Earth comes in the launching of Polar orbit satellites. The first six of these rockets launched by the United States from the California coast were full of disappointments and surprises. The first two, although perfect launchings, seemed to go wrong at the last minute, and although presumed to be in orbit, failed to show up on the first complete pass around the Earth. Technically speaking, they should have gone into orbit but they did not. Something happened, and the location of this something was the Polar area. The next two rockets fired did achieve orbits. This was done by "elevating sights", so to speak, and trying for a higher orbit, with a large degree of eccentricity, that is, a high point of orbit above the poles and a low point of orbit at equatorial areas. It was admitted that this eccentric orbit would produce a short-lived orbit, but it would also give the advantage of readings at widely varied heights above the Earth. Especially interesting was the readings expected above the Poles, because of the discovery of the radiation ring that surrounds the Earth like a huge doughnut, with openings at both Poles. Scientists were very anxious to map this area of low radiation, because it offered a hope of an escape breach for future space travelers who faced almost certain death from radiation while passing through the forbidding belt discovered around the equatorial and temperate areas of the Earth.

The next two satellites bore nose cones similar to those in which a future astronaut would be sent into orbit. In each one was a powerful radio transmitter, which was possible because the cone was the size of an automobile, and carried heavy batteries. Also included were powerful lights which could be illumi-nated at the proper time. The technique of releasing this cone from the satellite was to drop it by a radio-trig-gered device somewhere above Alaska. Once dropped, the cone lost altitude and proceeded around the Earth for one more revolution on its orbit. Having come over the Pole, it was then low enough (calculated the rocket men) to drop into the atmosphere over Hawaii, where a parachute would lower it slowly to the Earth's surface, and there huge planes awaited, rigged to "fish for" the descending cone, and take it to the plane before it dropped into the ocean and thus retrieve its important contents intact, without damage of crash landing.

On both occasions the following happened: The powerful radio signals were not heard at all. The lights were not seen at all. Radar, with a range at least 500 miles detected absolutely nothing. Each "pick-up" was a complete failure because there was nothing to pick up.

The explanation of the radio failure was advanced as "freezing" of the batteries so that the radio failed to work. No explanation was given for the failure of lights, or of radar detection. That the batteries froze is a strange explanation, considering that similar batteries in other satellites, orbiting for months, and even years, have never frozen. Failure might be admitted in one case, but total failure In both instances bears the aura of improbability.

Each launching was perfect. Orbits finely determined as to exact distance, speed, etc. were achieved, and constantly tracked. Yet, when the final deed is done, and the cone is detached successfully according to monitoring devices signaling the detachment, everything goes wrong and the result is complete and inexplicable disappearance of the cone. True, the statement is made that there is only a 1000 to 1 chance of success, and thus two failures are not unreasonable. But the failures are not to be complete ones. By failure is meant the successful final "pick-up" of the cone by the aircraft. Not complete disappearance! At least radio signals will be received, lights will be seen, radar will spot the descending cone.

Can it be that the reason the descending cone does not come over the Pole on that last low pass is because the Polar Area Is mysterious in extent, not in the area calculated by the rocket men, and therefore not taken into consideration? Can it be that the nose cone fell to Earth inside that "land of mystery" discovered by Admiral Byrd? Where else could they have gone? If the Earth at the Poles is as given on today's maps, could four successive "low-level" launchings give the same inexplicable result-unreasonable disappearance?

If there is 1700 (or more) miles of land extent in *addition* to the area bounded by longitudes and latitudes on a sphere existing in the Arctic, it follows that the recorded disappearances are not inexplicable, but *certain to occur!* Naturally a rocket cone figured to traverse a certain distance (in these cases approximately 33,000 miles) will not land at a predetermined point if the distance to be traveled is greater by 1700 miles. Our radar will fail to find our cone, and our eyes will see no lights. But why will our radio fail to send its signals to us? Is it because that "land of mystery" is of an "intervening" nature? Radio waves will not go through the Earth, of course. If solid substance intervenes, then we can understand why radio waves do not penetrate it. But what kind of a land configuration can it be that "intervenes" in this way? Why don't we have the "skip and bounce" effect from the stratosphere, which presumably exists over Byrd's "land of mystery" as well as over the lands on the map?

Since the mapped area of the spherical Earth does not allow sufficient room in which to place our two mystery lands, can it be that the Earth is of a different shape, one that allows us to place these lands on that portion of it which does not come under the category of "spherical": To many readers this will bring a snort and a humorous smile. They will say that we are bringing up the old saw of the Earth not being round. Columbus, they will say, finally proved that to the Earth's peoples, and Magellan actually did sail completely around the Earth by sailing in one direction until he had come back to his starting point. Also, anyone can go out on the night of a Lunar Eclipse, and see the round shadow of the Earth cross the face of the Moon. Seeing is believing, they will say-and just try to get around that!

It is true that seeing is believing, for most people. But the most informed optical scientist will not hold that popular view. He will point out that the human eye, like the telescope, is a lens. And the proved property of any lens is that it tends to make everything look round. No matter what we look at, distance converts the lines of the observed object from straight, or angular, or crooked, to perfectly circular one. This is a familiar phenomenon to aviators, who know that from the air, no house has a square chimney; they are all round. Any aircraft carrier pilot will tell you that as he brings in his Jet at a great height, his carrier looks like a round dot beneath him, and as he descends, it becomes a rectangle again. Anyone who has gone through a railroad tunnel, riding on the rear platform, will testify that the tunnel opening, if square, will gradually grow round as the train proceeds into the tunnel. Optical illusions, they are called. Any camera expert will tell you that the film records distant or extremely small objects as round dots, and that great magnification is necessary to resolve this roundness, and beyond a certain limit (that of the "grain" of the emulsion itself) it is impossible to resolve this roundness.

The scientific fact is that were the Moon actually square, at a distance of 240,000 miles our eye, our telescope, our camera would tell us it is round! No matter what shape it is, we would see it only as round. Actually, we cannot prove that the Moon is round; nor the Earth.

Thus, the arguments for a perfectly round Earth are not based on fact, only on assumption. This assumption is based on a brand of astronomy no longer acceptable to the scientist. Today the nebular theory of formation of planets, suns, even galaxies, is looked upon favorably. The condensation of nebula into stars and planets is accomplished by whirling motion. The whirling motion more often produces the "spindle" shape, round at the "equator", and projecting at the "pole"; or the "doughnut" shape, with flattened poles and holes through the middle. Since the Earth so formed, it may well be that it is either shape. We would not be aware of it by optical evidence, as we have shown.

On the one hand, the "spindle" shape possesses many specific arguments against it, and is the least reasonable. Astronomical bearings taken anywhere on the "spindle" portion would begin to show telltale evidence of the existence of the "spindle" shape. And they would be the reverse of factual sightings and bearings taken by Polar explorers. Actually, the bearings taken point to the "doughnut" shape.

Let us go back to Admiral Perry: his astounding rate of travel on his return from the Pole. If he were traveling over the inner lip of a "doughnut" shape, his bearings would indicate a great distance traveled, due to the fore-shortened horizon, and the "expanded" angle used in making his trigonometrical calculations. Actually he would be traveling the same distance each day, and the drop in speed would be entirely compatible with the bearing observations taken with a constantly lengthening horizon.

Rocket scientists have made much of the discovery of the Van Allen Belt, which is a belt of radiation surrounding the Earth. The reader is invited to read about it in *Scientific American,* and especially note the drawings of its shape, which are precisely a vast "doughnut", with the spherical Earth pictured at its center, in the "hole" of the doughnut. What if the Earth is not spherical, but actually doughnut-shaped, exactly as its surrounding Van Allen Belt? Whatever makes the belt thusly shaped, might it not also be responsible for shaping the Earth similarly?

The evidence is extremely strong, and amazingly prolific in scope and extent, that the Earth actually is shaped in this fashion. And if it is hollow, then we no longer need look for the saucers from outer space–but rather from 'inner space"! And judging from the evidences, the interior is extremely habitable! Vegetation in abundance is there; animals abound; the "extinct" mammoth still lives! Byrd flew 1700 miles over the inner edge of the "doughnut hole", and the Navy flew 2300 miles over the opposite inner edge. Both flights went a partial way into the inner Earth. And if this is all true, then no doubt extended flights to 10,000 miles and beyond have been made since 1957 into this hollow Earth, for we have the planes with the range to do it! If the government knew the significance of the Byrd-Navy flights, it would certainly not neglect to explore further!

Aime Michel, in his "straight line" theory, proved that most of the "flight patterns" of the flying saucers are on a north-south course, which is exactly what would be true if the origin of the saucers is Polar.

In the opinion of the editors of *Flying Saucers* this Polar origin of the flying saucers will now have to be factually disproved. It is completely necessary that this be done. More than a simple denial is necessary. Any denial must be accompanied with positive proof. *Flying Saucers* suggests that such proof cannot be provided. And until such proof is provided, *Flying Saucers* takes the stand that all saucer groups should study the matter from the hollow Earth viewpoint, amass all confirmatory evidence available in the last two centuries, and search diligently for any contrary evidence. Now that we have tracked the saucers to the most logical origin (the one we have consistently insisted must exist because of the insurmountable obstacle of interstellar origin which demands factors almost beyond imagination), that the saucers come from our own Earth, it must be proved or disproved, one way or the other.

Why? Because if the interior of the Earth is populated by a highly scientific and advanced race, we must make profitable contact with them; and if they are

110

mighty in their science, which includes the science of war, we must not make enemies of them; and if it is the intent of our governments to regard the interior of the Earth as "virgin territory", and comparable to the "Indian Territory" of North America when the settlers came over to take it away from its rightful owners, it is the right of the people to know that intent, and to express their desire in the matter.

The Flying Saucer has become the most important single fact in history. The answer to the questions raised in this article must be answered. Admiral Byrd has discovered a new and mysterious land, the center of the great unknown, and the most important discovery of all time. We have it from his own lips, from a man whose integrity has always been unimpeachable, and whose mind was one of the most brilliant of modern times.

Let those who wish to call him a liar step forward and prove their claim !

Flying saucers come from this Earth!

SHARULA

Part Nine
Secrets of the
Subterranean Cities

THE WORLD Ascension Network (360 Montezuma, Suite 221, Santa Fe, NM 87501) promotes the work of Sharula, princess of the underground city beneath Mt. Shasta. Here is the information they provided us on this famous entrance to the Inner Earth.

• • •

If you're reading this, chances are you haven't attended a meeting of the meeting of the Flat Earth Society lately. Since you know the Earth is round, consider the possibility that there is something inside of it, Not a sea of molten lava, but a network of polite subterraneans who have been waiting for the surface folk to get a clue. In one of our issues, we introduced you to the wonders of a world within a world. Following in the footsteps of Plato, Homer and Jules Verne...all believers in subterranean culture, we gave an overview of the social structure of the "Agartha Network". We told of Admiral Bird's wing camera documentation of the "holes at the poles," and of the U.S. government's elaborate expeditions and attempts to make contact. Back by popular demand, we are pleased to bring you a fur-

ther unveiling of life in the subterranean cities.

. . .

Recently, America watched Stephen Speilberg's TV pilot, a remake" of Verne's "Journey to the Center of the Earth." A maverick team of scientists aboard their melt-proof ship, enter the inner Earth through a bubbling volcano. When things cool off, they find themselves exploring a vast and sunny inner landscape...a magical and inviting world with ample room to fly.

Their adventure resembles the real life account of a Norwegian sailor named Olaf Jansen. His story, set in the 1800's, is told in Willis Emerson's biography entitled *The Smoky God* [which forms the first portion of this book–Editor]. Olaf's little sloop drifted so far north by storm, that he actually sailed into a polar entrance, and lived for two years with one of the colonies of the Agartha Network, called "Shamballa the Lesser". He describes his hosts as those "of the central seat of government for the inner continent...measuring a full 12 feet in height...extending courtesies and showing kindness...laughing heartily when they had to improvise chairs for my father and I to sit in." Olaf tells of a

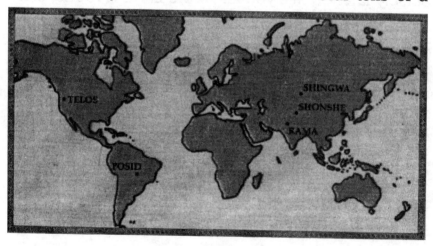

"smoky" inner sun, a world comprised of three fourths land and one fourth water.

The Agartha Network

Think of Shamballa the Lessor as the United Nations of over 100 subterranean cities that form the Agartha Network. It is indeed the seat of government for the inner world. While Shamballa the Lessor is an inner continent, its satellite colonies are smaller enclosed ecosystems located just beneath the Earth's crust or discreetly within mountains. All cities in the Agartha Network are physical, and are of the light, meaning that they are benevolent spiritually based societies who follow the Christic teachings of the Order of Meichizedek. Quite simply, they continue in the tradition of the great mystery schools of the surface, honoring such beings as Jesus/Sananda, Buddha, Isis and Osiris...all of the Ascended Masters that we of the surface know and love, in addition to spiritual teachers of their own longstanding heritage.

Why did they choose to live underground? Consider the magnitude of the geological Earth changes that have swept the surface over the past 100,000 years. Consider the lengthy Atlantean Lemurian war, and the power of thermo-nuclear weaponry that eventually sank and destroyed these two highly advanced civilizations. The Sahara, the Gobi, the Australian Outback, and the deserts of the U.S., are but a few examples of the devastation that resulted. The sub-cities were created as refuges for the people, and as safe havens for sacred records, teachings and technologies that were cherished by these ancient cultures.

Capitol Cities

POSID: Primary Atlantean outpost, located beneath

the Mato Grosso planes region of Brazil. Population: 1.3 million.

SHONSHE: Refuge of the Uighur culture, a branch of the Lemurians who chose to form their own colonies 50,000 years ago. Entrance is guarded by a Himalayan lamasary. Population ¾ million.

RAMA: Remnant of the surface city of Rama, India located near Jaipur. Inhabitants are known for their classic Hindu features. Population 1 million.

SHINGWA: Remnant of the northern migration of the Uighurs. Located on the border of Mongolia and China. Population ¾ million.

TELOS: Primary Lemurian outpost located within Mt. Shasta, with a small secondary city in Mt. Lassen, California, US. Telos translated means "communication with Spirit". Population 1.5 million.

Spotlight on Telos

Inquiring minds want to know how over a million people can make their home inside of Mt. Shasta.

While we're stretching our imaginations, our neighbors the Japanese have already blueprinted underground cities in an answer to their surface area problem. Subcity habitation has, for thousands of years, been a natural vehicle for human evolution. Now, here is a peek at a well thought out ecosystem.

The dimensions of this domed city are approximately 1.5 miles wide by 2 miles deep. Telos is comprised of 5 levels.

Level 1: This top level is the center of commerce, education and administration. The pyramid shaped temple is the central structure and has a capacity of 50,000. Surrounding it are government buildings, the equivalent of a courthouse that promotes an enlightened judicial system, halls of records, arts and entertainment facilities, a hotel for visiting foreign emissaries, a palace which houses the "Ra and Rana Mu" (the reigning King and Queen of the royal Lemurian lineage whom are Ascended Masters),a communications tower, a spaceport, schools, food and clothing dispatches, and most residences.

Level 2: A manufacturing center as well as a residential level. Houses are circular in shape, and dust free because of it. Like surface living, housing for singles, couples and extended families is the norm.

Level 3: Hydroponic gardens. Highly advanced hydroponic technology feeds the entire city with some to spare for inter-city commerce. All crops yield larger and tastier fruits, veggies and soy products that make for a varied and fun diet for Telosians. Now completely vegetarian, the Agartha Cities have taken meat substitutes to new heights.

Level 4: More hydroponic gardens, more manufacturing, some natural park areas.

Level 5: The nature level. Set about a mile beneath

117

surface ground level, this area is a large natural environment. It serves as a habitat for a wide variety of animals, including those many extinct on the surface. All species have been bred in a non-violent atmosphere, and those that might be carnivorous on the surface, now enjoy soy steaks, and human interaction. Here you can romp with a Sabor Tooth Tiger with wild abandon. Together with the other plant levels, enough oxygen is produced to sustain the biosphere.

LANGUAGE: While dialects vary from city to city, "Solara Maru" translated as the "Solar Language, "is commonly spoken. This is the root language for our sacred languages such as Sanskrit and Hebrew.

GOVERNMENT: A Council of Twelve, six men and six women, together with the Ra and Rana Mu, do collective problem solving and serve as guides and guardians of the people. Positions of royalty, such as are held by the Ra and Rana Mu are regarded as ones of responsibility in upholding God's divine plan. The High Priest, an Ascended Master named Adama, is also an official representative.

COMPUTERS: The Agarthean computer system is amino-acid based, and serves a vast array of functions. All of the sub-cities are linked by this highly spiritualized information network. The system monitors inter-city and galactic communication, while simultaneously serving the needs of the individual at home. It can, for instance, report your body's vitamin or mineral deficiencies, or when necessary, convey pertinent information from the akashic records for personal growth.

MONEY: Non-existent. All inhabitants basic needs are taken care of. Luxuries are exchanged via a sophisticated barter system.

TRANSPORTATION: Moving sidewalks, inter-level elevators, and electromagnetic sleds resembling our snow mobiles within the city. For travel between cities, residents take "the Tube", an electromagnetic subway system capable of speeds up to 3,000 mph. Yes, Agartheans are well versed in inter-galactic etiquette, and are members of the Confederation of Planets. Space travel has been perfected, as has the ability for inter-dimensional shifts that render these ships undetectable.

ENTERTAINMENT: Theatre, concerts, and a wide variety of the arts. Also, for you Trekkies, the Holodecks. Program your favorite movie or chapter in Earth history, and become a part of it!

CHILDBIRTH: A painless three months, not nine. A very sacred process whereby upon conception, a woman will go to the temple for three days, immediately welcoming the child with beautiful music, thoughts and imagery. Water birthing in the company of both parents is standard.

HEIGHT: Due to cultural differences, average heights of subterranean citizens vary. Generally 6'5" to 7'5" in Telos while nearly 12' in Shamballa the Lessor.

AGE: Unlimited. Death by degeneration is simply not a reality in Telos. Most Agartheans choose to look an age between 30 and 40, and stay there, while technically they may be thousands of years old. By not believing in death, this society is not limited by it. Upon completing a desired experience, one can disincarnate at will.

ASCENSION: Absolutely, and much easier and more common than on the surface. Ascension is the ultimate goal of temple training.

Why have they stayed underground all this time? In part, because the Agartheans have learned the futility of war and violence, and are patiently waiting for us to draw the same conclusion. They are such gentle folk, that even our judgmental thoughts are physically harmful to them. Secrecy has been their protection. Until now, the truth of their existence has been veiled by Spirit.

When can we visit? Our entrance to the sub-cities depends on the purity of our intentions, and our capacity to think positive. A warm welcome from both worlds is the ideal, and must be expressed by more than just the lightworking community.

Currently, a few hundred brave subterraneans are working on the surface. In order to blend with the masses, they have undergone temporary cellular change, so that physically, they don't tower above the rest of us. They may be recognized by their gentle, sensitive nature, and somewhat mysterious accent. We wish to introduce you to a very special one of them. Her name is Princess Sharula Aurora Dux. The daughter of the Ra and Rana Mu of Telos, Sharula has been officially appointed Ambassador to the surface world by the Agartha Network. She is 267 years old, and looks 30. All of the above is courtesy of her first hand experience. Sharula, currently known to thousands, shall soon be known to millions.

The purpose of her Ambassadorship is to prepare the way for the merging of the two worlds...to bring the ideas, the information and the new archetypes that will help unite our planet. Sharula has come to present a blueprint for peaceful change to those who will listen. *Now, the Agartheans have reached a point where they cannot progress spiritually unless this merger takes place. In essence, we are one planet ascending, not half a planet. It is God's will that we take the next step together.* The sooner we invite this unity, the sooner the magic will unfold. The Hierarchy has made the emergence of the subterranean cities a priority project. They are asking us to do our part in welcoming our brethren. The timing depends very much upon our receptivity and our graciousness. A successful merger is estimated within the next 10 to 20 years. *Beloved, there is nothing to fear, and everything to gain.* The gifts the Agartheans bring are many. The secret of immortality is also your birthright., The freedom to live in abundance is also your birthright. You haven't lived until you've tasted a hydroponic tomato, and by all means, a little fun on the Holodeck should be had by all.

Introducing the Woman from Telos, the City Beneath Mount Shasta–Sharula

The following interview with Sharula took place on July 23, 1990, and is reprinted from *Insights For Positive Living.* She shares with us some wonderful information about the Atlantean and Lemurian cities that exist beneath the earth's surface.

She speaks from her home, Telos, a city built a mile or so beneath Mt. Shasta, California. During a recent trip to Mt. Shasta, I encountered several local townspeople who had personally seen mysterious fires and lights on the slopes of Mt. Shasta, and have heard otherworldly chants and music late at night, emanating from the mountain. And of course, there have been sightings of mysterious robed people walking into the side of the mountain. Even the local visitor's guide mentions the Lemurian connection to Mt. Shasta!

This interview may really stretch your perception of reality. I hope it does. It's meant to. Sharula is Love and I am delighted to share her story with you.

INSIGHTS: *Let's start off with some basic questions of who you are and where you are from.*

SHARULA: My name is Sharula and I come from a city underneath Mt. Shasta, called Telos. The city was constructed about 14,000 years ago at the termination of the Lemurian continent. When the scientists and priests of Lemuria realized the continent was about to sink, they petitioned a group called the Agharta Network, which controlled all the subterranean cities, to build our own city beneath Mt. Shasta.

There was an original set of caverns there. We chose to enlarge these caverns to make them bigger and more livable.

INSIGHTS: *How large is Telos?*

SHARULA: It's on five different levels. The bottom level is about 1½ miles across, the other levels are different. The closest level to the mountain itself is only about three-quarters of a mile across.

INSIGHTS: *How many people live in Telos?*

SHARULA: A million and a half.

INSIGHTS: *Tell us about your ecosystem; your water, food, air environment–what is it like to live in Telos?*

SHARULA: We have perpetual light through a process of energizing stones to create full spectrum lighting. We process them with the forces that makes them small suns.

The five levels are garden levels where we produce all the food we need with hydroponic gardens. There are plants on all five levels that continue to circulate the air. We work off the same system the earth does, the plants produce oxygen. Plus, we have air shafts that come through the surface that sends air. Since that air is polluted, we use them less and less.

INSIGHTS: *What form of government do you have?*

SHARULA: We have a system where the government is run by a council of twelve plus one. They are twelve masters, six male and six female. If anyone has a disagreement, they go to an arbitrator, rather than fight it out among themselves. All arbitrators report to the council and they change constantly. They are appointed to that position based on their natural affinity for it.

INSIGHTS: *Who appoints them to that position?*

SHARULA: The temple is run by the Melchezidek. Those in the temple, the high priests and high priestesses, are all ascended, therefore they are all working totally off God Consciousness, so that the human ego does not interfere at all with anything they do.

INSIGHTS: *You mentioned that they are of Melchezidek?*

SHARULA: All through the cosmos, there is an order called the Melchezidek. These are the beings who, through incarnation after incarnation, are the priests, the ones who've chosen to serve God, no matter what the guide might look like. They have donated their spiritual growth towards serving the Will of God. They are the cosmic priesthood you might say. There are several Melchezidek focuses on the planet at this time, one of them is the temple of Mt. Shasta.

INSIGHTS: *You mean underneath Mt. Shasta?*

SHARULA: Not only underneath is there the physical temple inside the city, but there is an ethereal temple that crowns Mt. Shasta. There's also a major Melchezidek retreat over Cuba which is run by one of the Archangels. And there's a Melchezidek retreat in Egypt.

INSIGHTS: *And these are all in the etheric?*

SHARULA: No, the one in Egypt is ethereal and in the physical also. There's one over South America and one in Moto Grosso, which is physical and that is where the Atlantean city is, in the Brazilian jungle.

INSIGHTS: *Earlier, you mentioned that when your city was formed 14,000 years ago, you hade to petition*

*the Agartha, the ones in charge of the inner earth cities.
Are there other cities in existence?*

SHARULA: Oh, yes. There are many. There are
over one hundred inner earth cities. Some of them are
very similar. The major one is called "Shamballa The
Lesser." It's been in existence for a half million years. It
was formed by a group of people called Hyprobeans or
Trypoleans.

INSIGHTS: *Where is Shamballa located?*

SHARULA: It's at the center of the planet itself. In
spite of what scientists have told people, it is not a raging ball of fire.

INSIGHTS: *How does one travel from city to city or
from surface to inner city?*

SHARULA: Probably the most common method is
what we call the "tubes." It is a series of underground
trains. We've bored tunnels that run underneath all the
oceans and all the continents and connect all the cities
and several of the retreats. The trains, which look very
much like a subway train, are run on a cushion of air,
an electromagnetic cushion, so they never actually
touch the sides of the tunnel. This cushion creates a
force field without friction and therefore they can
achieve very high speeds. The trains are capable of running over 3,000 mph.

INSIGHTS: *Between the surface and the inner
cities, how does one travel?*

SHARULA: There are several entrances that open to
the surface. We'll use a ship which is run by the Silver
Fleet.

INSIGHTS: *The Silver Fleet...explain that please.*

SHARULA: We are under the Ashtar Command
and within this command are several fleets. The fleets
native to Earth are the Silver Fleet. Earth is called a
fallen planet, simply because it's fallen into the third

dimension and consciousness and has remained there. The Silver Fleet is made up of beings from the Agarthean cities. Many of the ships that people see in the air are silver fleets ships, except for the "nasties."

INSIGHTS: *How can one identify a Silver Fleet ship as opposed to the "nasties," as you call them?*

SHARULA: All the Ashtar Command ships, all the Confederation ships run from divine geometrics. The ships will be either cylinder or they will be saucer shaped or they will be round. There are *not* a lot of protrusions and angles; they have a tendency to be smooth. The ships that come in boomerang shapes and other weird configurations are usually not Confederation ships.

INSIGHTS: *Let's talk about the people themselves, the Telosians. What would a typical Telosian look like?*

SHARULA: The typical Telosian has a slightly golden tone to his skin and has a tendency toward high cheek bones and slightly almond-shaped eyes. Most Telosians run toward light hair and we have all eye colors. The men are generally 7' to 7'6" in height and the women are generally 6'6" to 7'1" in height. When we come to the surface we have a process of altering the molecules in our bodies so that we are able to appear the same height as people here on the surface.

INSIGHTS: *Does your civilization have any of the social problems that ours seems to have, like: pollution, hunger, homeless people and water droughts?*

SHARULA: No. We don't have pollution because we are able to monitor our systems at all times. We have learned to accelerate the atom. When the first scientists started working with atoms they didn't realize that they weren't meant to shatter the atom for energy; they were meant to accelerate the atom for energy that won't die out and won't produce hazardous afterform. Because we learned to accelerate the atoms, we're also able to dematerialize all of our waste matter and return it back to its original form, which is the divine ethers in non-material state.

INSIGHT: *Please share with us about how the women of Telos give birth to their children.*

SHARULA: We have returned the process of child-birth to divine order. Women in third dimensional bodies were only meant to bear children in three months; it was not meant to be a nine month process. Even now a fetus is formed in three months. When a woman realizes that she is pregnant, she goes instantly into the temple and for 24 hours she is sealed in a chamber that produces absolutely nothing but beautiful images, beautiful sounds, beautiful thoughts and she is constantly told how beautiful she is and how perfect her child is. So, the very start of this life is impregnated in all the cells of their being with how perfect and how loved they are.

After three months, she returns to a birth chamber and a high priestess will put the mother in a slight altered state whereas she feels no pain, she's just happy and euphoric.

All the births take place underwater, which produces almost no labor pains. The mother feels nothing but pressure, she's not going through trauma. Because the mother is relaxed, the baby goes through less physical pain. When the baby is born in the water, both parents are there to hold it. They allow the baby to float underwater for some time until the baby itself chooses to come to the surface and breathe. And because there is no trauma about breathing, the baby has also learned to take complete breaths and they're not shut off immediately by panic and pain.

INSIGHTS: *Is the U.S. Government aware of the*

existence of Telos and the other underground cities?

SHARULA: Yes. For a long time they have been trying to get in, to access the information of Telos and the Silver Fleet. The promise of what they need would be given to them, but in return there are several things they have to do or quit doing.

INSIGHTS: *What was it that they were given to do or stop doing?*

SHARULA: Basically, return the country to what it was founded on, and return to an open and honest government, so that every citizen has access to what's happening in the government.

INSIGHTS: *Are you referring to the government's interaction with other extraterrestrials that are not of the Silver Fleet?*

SHARULA: Yes, that is only one.

INSIGHTS: *When was the government first introduced to Telos?*

SHARULA: They have been aware of the subterranean cities and they have been aware of Telos since the country's conception. It is only near the turn of the century that they started taking action. This action did not get real aggressive until the 1950s.

INSIGHTS: *In wrapping up, is there a special message that you'd like to share with our readers?*

SHARULA: We have come up for a reason. We are not here for sightseeing. We have information that we are releasing to the people up here. Information on how to achieve the state of mastery, the state called ascension, how to return back to their God-Self. We want to teach more and more people up here how to achieve freedom, where they are no longer tied to anything. Right now, I'm in the process of writing a book and I give workshops. My husband, Shield, and I are twin flames and we are achieving workshops around the country to help people to some of these processes. We're starting with the more simple knowledge which will lead to the more advanced. We are releasing the information that our people have been guarding for all these thousands of years.

It is the goal of the Hierarchy of this planet to unite the inner and the outer, as the inner cities and the outer cities become one. There are a few things that have to happen before that. We must achieve through our ambassadorships the exchange of information to awaken people to their potential, their Godhood, to their impending mastery. When the unification comes, the people in the outside cities will hold the same consciousness as the people in the inner cities.

Part Ten
Aliens & Atlanteans of Mount Shasta

by Commander X

According to the author of *Underground Alien Bases* and *The Ultimate Deception,* there are at last count over 50 such bases being occupied by both "good" and "bad" ETs in the U.S. alone. One of the most active is to be found in Northern California.

• • •

One of the UFO underground bases the "good guys" are definitely in control of, is the base beneath Mt. Shasta in northern California.

The tunnels under Mt. Shasta are vast and house equipment and ships you wouldn't believe could possibly exist. There are teleportation and levitation devices, huge (by our definition) "Mother-Ships," and a crystal almost the size of a New York City skyscraper.

From all over the globe, hundreds of New Agers visit this site annually, and some even make this their home. Quite a number of "space channels," are known to operate in the area, such as Sister Thedra, who has been channeling Ashtar as well as other Space Guardians, not to mention Count Saint Germain, who has been known to visit here in his physical body from time to time.

Mt. Shasta is rich in the lore of the occult and metaphysics. It is truly a spiritual focal point for this planet. Deep from beneath the ground–where only the most aware are allowed–a full-time operation is constantly being carried out to save the Earth.

I have been told by sources whom I trust completely that the base was originally established by the people of Lemuria, a great continent that once existed in the middle of the Pacific; but just like its sister continent Atlantis, was destroyed due to the greedy nature and negativity of a few foolish leaders who were bent on planetary–as well as interplanetary conquest.

So many "odd and peculiar" happenings have transpired around and in Mount Shasta that it would take several volumes to even penetrate the surface of all this material. The Lemurians–some of whom still reside here are often seen wandering in the region. They can be recognized due to the fact that they are quite tall-in the eight and nine foot range. They even have their own underground city here, and it's all made of gold. Even the nature spirits–the knomes, the elves and the fairies-run about here non-disturbed, and many "outsiders" will tell you that they've heard the sound of far away flutes, which are the favorite instrument of the elemental kingdom. The only "unusual dweller" around these parts I might be the least bit cautious of would be our hairy friend Bigfoot, who has been known to scare the living hell out of hikers who go away not being such "happy campers," mainly due to the somewhat non-appealing scent he has been known to toss off.

I've been told that Mt. Shasta has a highly charged aura which prevents the forces of darkness from penetrating anywhere nearby. Teams of Lemurians, Space Brothers and elementals working jointly, meditate daily underground here to heal the planet and to keep this sacred spot safe from either physical or mental attack. Those that have been in the tunnels underground are never the same, their whole life so changed by what they have seen and heard!

There is even one instance that I know of where a young woman–just recently married–was healed by the rays of a space ship that hovered over her small camp. Hanna Spitzer told her amazing story in an old issue of Tim Beckley's UFO Review, from which I have his permission to quote excerpts:

"My husband, Damian, and I came to Mt. Shasta just last September. We were drawn here by the majesty that surrounds this area. Damian had been here before and so he was familiar with the surrounding communities and the people who reside near this locale.

"Our closest friend, Patrick, a very talented young artist, had been my husband's companion on his earlier visit, and he also was captivated with Mt. Shasta. As luck had it, he was to be commissioned by a local restaurant owner to paint a huge mural of Mt. Shasta and the many legends that have long surrounded this magical mountain.

"Quickly, we moved up the side of the mountain and set up camp. From here we had a picturesque view of Mt. Shasta City. This tiny village consists of ski shops and sleepy little hide-a-ways, with a few occult bookstores and health food stores thrown in for good measures. At one of the stores, someone told us about a strange light that had been seen while this person was out camping on the same property where we were living. Apparently, she awoke from a deep sleep and saw numerous flashing lights and heard a whooping noise.

When she went into town the next morning she found that others had undergone similar experiences.

"Throughout our stay, Patrick kept telling us about a wonderful lady, a very gifted psychic, who was said to be a real 'powerhouse,' and who could attract a lot of phenomenon herself. Her name was Aendreious, and Patrick had invited her to come and stay with all of us. I was really fascinated by what I had heard, and couldn't wait to meet this woman.

"One day when Damian was in town doing some chores a striking woman in a turban approached him. It was Aendreious. Damian brought her up to the land that afternoon and immediately we were struck by her presence. As gifts, she had brought each of us a crystal. She spoke in a very knowing manner. On top of this, she was very meditative and peaceful and extremely fascinated with the mountain. Through this lady we learned quite a lot about magnetism and attraction. I knew–as we all did–that if we were to have a sighting, it would be while she was living with us.

"Aendreious had a wonderful attitude about flying saucers and aliens. She thought of them as masters, not little green men to be afraid of. Her talking calmed me a bit and I soon lost any fear I might have had. For days the men had been teasing me about the dark and about creatures who would try to grab me and take me away.

"Going into town became an experience in itself. We loved to speak with the people there and hear about their experiences first hand. There was one charming lady who walked through the streets talking to everyone she met about the saucers. She always wore a shiny yellow hat and seemed very devoted to her task."

. . .

William E Hamilton III–Bill to just about anyone who knows him–became fascinated with the mystery of Mt. Shasta after reading the book *A Dweller on Two Planets,* by Phylos. This was even before his first visit to the mountain which–believe it or not–took place when he was just 15 years old.

I would suppose it was sometime later, however, that Bill actually began to look into the rumors and stories regarding underground bases which are known to crisscross this country–not to mention the rest of the world!

Then finally in 1977, the veteran researcher whose work is highly respected by other UFOlogists, had a first-hand encounter with a young woman who sent his mind whirling and his thoughts buzzing. For this attractive, but very exotic looking lady revealed that she was not a full time inhabitant of our world, but was actually a resident of an underground city located at the very heart of Mt. Shasta. Extracts of what she revealed to Bill regarding her subterranean domain, and her people's origins, their ongoing contact with outer space beings, was all part of their conversation which took place during several meetings. The woman's story–as you will see in just a moment–is utterly fascinating and deserves the attention of anyone doing serious research into underground cities and bases.

. . .

The Girl From Beneath Mt. Shasta

I run across some fascinating people in the course of my investigations who tell me many unusual stories. While on the trail of reports of UFO base locations, I met a young, very pretty blonde girl with almond-shaped eyes and small perfect teeth, whose name was Bonnie. Bonnie has told me an incredible story and has related a volume of interesting information on Atlantis and Lemuria. Bonnie is sincere, cheerful, and rational, and says she is a Lemurian born under the sign of Leo in 1951 in a city called Telos that was built inside an artificial dome-shaped cavern in the Earth a mile or so beneath Mt. Shasta, California.

Bonnie, her mother, her father Ramu, her sister Judy, her cousins Lorae and Matox, live and move in our society, returning frequently to Telos for rest and recuperation.

Bonnie relates that her people use boring machines to bore tunnels in the Earth. These boring machines heat the rock to incandescence, then vitrify it, thus eliminating the need for beams and supports.

A tube transit train system is used to connect the few Atlantean/Lemurian cities that exist in various subterranean regions of our hemisphere. The tube trains are propelled by electromagnetic impulses up to speeds of 2500 mph. One tube connects with one of their cities in the Mato Grosse jungle of Brazil. The Lemurians have developed space travel and some flying saucers come from their subterranean bases. Bonnie says her people are members of a federation of planets.

They grow food hydrophonically under full-spectrum lights with their gardens attended by automatons. The food and resources of Telos are distributed in plenty to the million-and-a-half population that thrives on a no-money economy. Bonnie talks about history, of the Uighers, Naga-Mayas, and Quetzels, of which she is a descendant. She recounts the destruction of Atlantis and Lemuria and of a war between the two superpowers fought with advanced weaponry: She says the

Atlanteans built a huge crystal-powered beam weapon that was used to control a small moon of Earth as a missile to be aimed at China, but their plans went awry and the moon split in two, coming down into the Atlantic, north of Bermuda, deluging the remaining isle of Atlantis. She claims her people are now part of a much greater underground kingdom called Agharta-ruled by a super race she calls "Hyprobeans."

I met Bonnie's cousin, Matox, who, like her, is a strict vegetarian and holds the same attitudes concerning the motives of government. They constantly guard against discovery or intrusion. Their advanced awareness and technology helps them to remain vigilant. Will we openly meet these long-lost relatives of ours? Bonnie says yes, but this is part of her incredible mission. Her mission: to warn those who will listen of the coming cataclysms that will culminate at the end of the century in a shift of the Earth's axis. After this catastrophe, she says the world will be one, and the survivors will build a new world free of worry, poverty, disease and exploitation. The world will exist on a higher plane of vibrations and man will come to know his true history and heritage.

Science fiction? Bonnie is a real person. Many have met her. Is she perpetrating a hoax? For what motive? She does not seek publicity and I had a devil of a time getting her to meetings to talk with others, but she has done so. There has been little variation in her story or her answers in the past three years. She has given me excellent technical insight on the construction of a crystal-powered generator that extracts ambient energy. She has given me new insights on UFOs and their purpose in coming here. Bonnie's father, the Ramu, is 300 years old and a member of the ruling council of Telos.

Many tunnels are unsafe and closed off. All tube

transit tunnels are protected and are designed to eject uninvited guests. Does Bonnie have the answers that we are looking for? I don't know. I am not making the claims nor can I provide proof. Bonnie says she would like to satisfy our need for proof and will work with me on a satisfactory answer to that problem, but she is unconcerned with whether people accept her or not. Bonnie is humorous and easy-going and well-poised, yet sometimes she becomes brooding and mysterious. She says her people are busy planning survival centers for refugees. One of these is to be near Prescott, Arizona.

Following is a question and answer session between Mr. Hamilton and Bonnie, which was done to answer even more questions about this underground world we are so intrigued by:

Q. *Were there ten races on Lemuria?*

A. They were called sub-races. There was only one race.

Q: *Can you date that?*

A. That was approximately 200,000 years ago.

Q. *You once said that the early Lemurians come from the planet Aurora?*

A. Yes, and at that time the sun (of Earth) was giving off entirely too much radiation, resulting in shorter live spans. The Hyprobeans went inside this planet. They entered at the polar entrances, inside of which there is another sun which has no radioactive effect. These people still live there in the major city of Shamballa. They are still ruled by the hereditary King of the World. The people who remained on top degenerated into what we call the Fourth Race.

Q. *Did they continue to degenerate?*

A. They continued to degenerate. There came to be more differences in the races. They started mental degeneration on the point of warring on each other.

136

Before, fighting was unheard of.

Q. *Did they have technology at that time?*

A. At that time, the technology was quite high. The Lemurians started in stature from about 12 feet to about nine feet. The fourth race was about nine feet tall. The people started taking on the color of the land. The Atlantean skins were taking on a reddish hue. Asian and Lemurian skins took on a yellowish hue. (Note: Adam means red-man!)

Q. *OK, so we had some kind of war going on at that time?*

A. Right!...The fourth race. We started to degrade into the fifth race at the time the war started, approximately 25,000 years ago. At this time Atlantis chose to break away from the Motherland Mu. Atlantis was getting more and more vindictive. They were living under the Law of the One-the One God. The Lemurians were the major race at this time which had developed into the Uighers, the Naga Mayas, and the Quetzelcoatls. The Quetzels at this time started leaving Lemuria in droves.

Q. *Where did they go?*

A. To North America, then on to the Scandinavian countries. Some of them went south into Central and South America and some of the descendants are still there. Explorers have brought back records of white Indians (true).

Q. *Do you know who Quetzeicoatl and Viracocha were?*

A. Quetzelcoatl was Venusian. Viracocha was a Lemurian High Priest who went to South America upon the destruction of Lemuria.

Q. *What sent Lemuria to the bottom—a war or natural catastrophe?*

A. It was the blowing out of Archean gas chambers.

When the Earth was forming, huge gas pockets were formed, cavities within the Earth, some of which were just a few feet wide, but thousands of miles long. The scientists started detecting the weakening of the Archean gas chambers on their instruments. This was about 15,000 years ago and at that time the Earth's magnetic field was getting very erratic.

Q. *Did you have contact with extraterrestrials at that time?*

A. At that time we were still in contact with the Federation. Lemuria and Atlantis were both members of the Federation.

Q. *Did they have air travel and space travel?*

' A. Yes, they did. Atlantis and Lemuria could both travel to other planets.

Q. What was it that destroyed Atlantis?

A. After the destruction of Lemuria, which was caused by natural catastrophe, for a long time the planet was unstable, for about 200 or 300 years. The pyramids were built before the destruction of Lemuria. At this time the Atlanteans were becoming difficult and several of them who believed in the Law of the One did not care for what the scientists were doing. The scientists were experimenting with monster crystals that had unbelievable power.

Q. *Were there any biological experiments like cloning or with DNA?*

A. Yes, there were. This had been going on for hundreds of years by that time. They were using the "things" as their slaves. Some people left Atlantis at this time and came to Mt. Shasta where the Lemurians had built a city called Telos.

Q. *Now the Atlanteans started experimenting with huge crystals–were these the fire crystals?*

A. Yes, they generated cosmic energy. It is the cut of

the crystal which causes the generation (wavelength?). It draws out of the atmosphere (the energy) and generates it into a high force and higher vibration. It has no moving parts. The crystal has an inner fire-they change colors. The crystals the Atlanteans used built up energy they could not control.

Q. *Is this the secret of the power source on flying saucers?*

A. Yes, a lot of it is crystals, particularly the atmospheric vehicles. The planet-to-planet vehicles are driven by an Ion-Mercury engine. Spaceships can reach speeds way beyond light-they can enter hyperspace you generate into the fourth dimension-this is controlled by an onboard computer that takes you into and out of hyperspace. I know this is a simplification. When you're on a ship going into hyperspace, you will hear this vibration and a loud screaming sound when you enter, then you will hear nothing. (I have had many correlations on this data and am researching it further toward a comprehensive theory of space travel).

Q. *Do you travel between galaxies?*

A. Yes, that is usually when you enter hyperspace when you are going a far, far distance.

Q. *Have you heard stories of any advanced beings out there?*

A. Yes, they are near the center of the Universe.

Q. *What is at the Center?*

A. We call it the seat of God-the generation of energy.

• • •

William Hamilton should be congratulated on his being such an energetic and dedicated seeker of truth in this field. He has spent tireless hours without thought of remuneration and has personally neglected

THE SMOKY GOD & OTHER INNER EARTH MYSTERIES

any fanfare in order to pierce through the fog of misin-
formation that is so often placed in our path. Those
interested in finding out more about Bill's work can
write the publisher for information on his privately
published manuscript *Alien Magic*, and his group,
UFORCES.

Certainly, he is one of those who can testify that the
truth will set *us all* free!

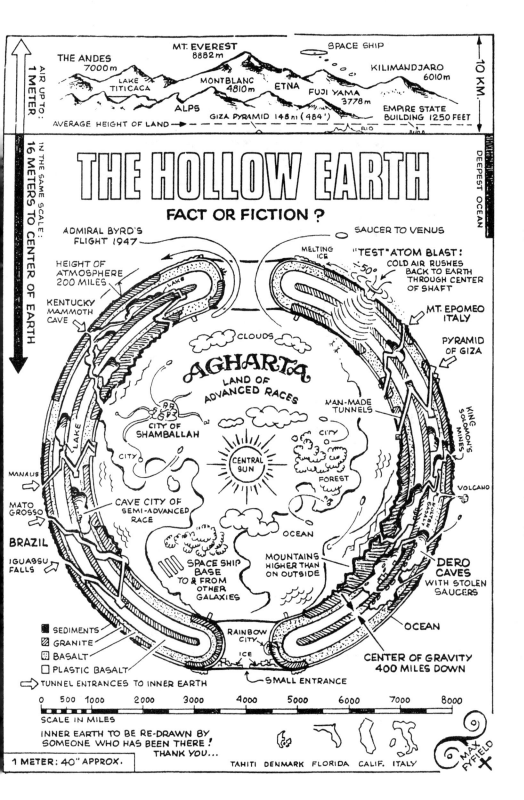

Danish artist Max Fyfield shows subsurface layers and the wide range of beings who inhabit the inner Earth.

OTHER TITLES OF INTEREST

OTHER BOOKS OF INTEREST FROM
INNER LIGHT

THE ULTIMATE DECEPTION—by Commander X
Has the U.S. military formulated a secret agreement with the alien group known as the Greys and what is their sinister purpose and plan for the future of Earth? Here are "inside" stories from those in the military who have lived this great threat for many days of their lives—

UNDERGROUND ALIEN BASES—by Commander X
Here is a "Secret Report" on the location of many of these underground bases said to exist in the United States, including Dulce, Mt. Shasta, Brown Mountain, Superstition Mountains. Here also are the stories by those few who have gained entrance to these bases and lived to tell exactly what it is they have seen underground. Includes thrilling revelations by UFO abductee Christa Tilton and others.—

MJ-12 & THE RIDDLE OF HANGAR 18—by Timothy Green Beckley
Here is the shocking evidence that the government actually possesses the remains of crashed UFOs and the bodies of aliens found onboard these extraterrestrial ships. Published for the first time are many FBI, CIA and State Department documents that offer proof that aliens have arrived on our cosmic shores and that the White House knows exactly what is going on.—

THE UFO SILENCERS—MYSTERY OF THE MEN IN BLACK—
by Timothy Green Beckley
One by one these strange "Men in Black" have warned witnesses to remain silent! Who are these MIB who have become so much a part of unexplained aerial phenomena? Are they military agents? Do they represent a "Secret Government"? Or are they ETs themselves? Here are reports and stories so bizarre that they defy any sort of ordinary explanation.—

UFO CRASH SECRETS AT WRIGHT PATTERSON AIR FOR BASE—
by James W. Moseley
What is inside the mysterious "Hangar 18" at the Air Technology Center at Wright Patterson, and why has even Senator Barry Goldwater not been allowed to enter this Top Secret facility? The author is one of the few UFOlogists actually to have ever been permitted access to the base. What he found out about the strange happenings there are startling. To be published summer of 1991. Advance publication price—

Order From:
INNER LIGHT PUBLICATIONS
P.O. Box 753 (CS)
New Brunswick, NJ 08903

NJ residents add sales tax. Allow 4–6 weeks for delivery.

Published by:
**INNER LIGHT PUBLICATIONS,
Box 753, New Brunswick, NJ 08903**

Free catalog upon request.